LOVE POEMS OF
SIX CENTURIES

LOVE POEMS OF SIX CENTURIES

Edited by Helen Husted

INTRODUCTION BY WILLIAM ROSE BENÉT

DECORATIONS BY LEE MARIL

Granger Index Reprint Series

BOOKS FOR LIBRARIES PRESS

FREEPORT, NEW YORK

Copyright, 1950 By Coward-McCann, Inc.
Reprinted 1969 by arrangement

STANDARD BOOK NUMBER:
8369-6105-6

LIBRARY OF CONGRESS CATALOG CARD NUMBER:
70-86798

MANUFACTURED
BY
HALLMARK LITHOGRAPHERS, INC.
IN THE U.S.A.

COPYRIGHT ACKNOWLEDGMENTS

Arranged Alphabetically by Authors

Walter Benton, 79, 181

"Entry April 28" and "Entry November 12" from *This Is My Beloved* by Walter Benton. Copyright, 1943, by Alfred A. Knopf, Inc. Reprinted by permission of the publisher.

The Bible, 147, 149, 151

"The Song of Solomon," sections IV, V, and VII.

Laurence Binyon, 16

"O World, Be Nobler" from *Collected Poems*. Reprinted by permission of The Society of Authors, London, and Mrs. Binyon.

William Blake, 47, 109, 159

✗ Song"; "Never Seek to Tell Thy Love"; from "Lament of Ahania"

Robert Bridges, 17, 240, 252

From "Indolence: XII"; "The Garden in September"; and "Song" in *Shorter Poems* by Robert Bridges. Reprinted by permission of The Clarendon Press, Oxford.

John Malcolm Brinnin, 108

"A Letter" from *The Garden Is Political*. Copyright, 1942, by John Malcolm Brinnin. Used by permission of The Macmillan Company.

Emily Brontë, 226

"Remembrance"

Rupert Brooke, 98

"The Hill" from *The Collected Poems of Rupert Brooke*. Copyright, 1915, by Dodd, Mead & Company, Inc. Reprinted by permission of Dodd, Mead & Company, Inc. and McClelland & Stewart Ltd., Toronto.

William Browne, 60

"Song"

Elizabeth Barrett Browning, 177, 261, 269

From "Sonnets from the Portuguese"

Robert Browning, 20, 28, 132, 256

"Song"; "Meeting at Night"; "A Woman's Last Word"; from "By the Fireside"

Edward George Bulwer-Lytton, 183

"Absent Yet Present"

Edward Robert Bulwer-Lytton, 206

"The Last Wish"

Robert Burns, 8, 58, 191

"I'm Owre Young to Marry Yet"; "A Red, Red Rose"; and "Farewell to Nancy"

Witter Bynner, 271, 273

"Songs Ascending" and "Night" from *Collected Poems* by Witter Bynner. Copyright, 1920, by Alfred A. Knopf, Inc.; copyright,

1948, by Witter Bynner. Reprinted by permission of the publisher.

George Noël Gordon, Lord Byron, 189, 194, 208
"We'll Go No More A-Roving"; "When We Two Parted"; and "Farewell!"

Thomas Campion, 122, 161
"Sleep, Angry Beauty"; and "If Thou Longst So Much to Learn"

Thomas Carew, 144
"Secrecy Protested"

William Cartwright, 104
"To Chloe"

William Cavendish, 243
"Love's Vision"

Geoffrey Chaucer, 6, 43, 69
"To Rosémounde, A Ballad"; "Merciles Beaute: III, Escape"; and "Song of Troilus"

Richard Church, 92
"In a Woman's Face." Reprinted by permission of the author and J. M. Dent and Sons Ltd., London.

John Clare, 211
"Thou Flower of Summer"

William Corkine, 36
"Sweet, Let Me Go!"

Frances Cornford, 170
"Dawn." Reprinted by permission of the author.

John Cornford, 135
"To Margot Heinemann" from *John Cornford: A Memoir*, edited by Pat Sloan; published by Jonathan Cape Ltd., London. Reprinted by permission of The Student Labour Federation of Great Britain.

Charles Cotton, 129
"Virelay"

Donah Maria (Mulock) Craik, 224
"Douglas"

Countee Cullen, 54
"A Song of Praise" from *Color* by Countee Cullen. Copyright, 1925, by Harper & Bros. Reprinted by permission of the publisher.

E. E. Cummings, 62
"Somewhere I Have Never Travelled" from *Collected Poems*, published by Harcourt, Brace and Company, Inc. Copyright, 1931, by E. E. Cummings. Reprinted by permission of Brandt & Brandt.

viii

Leigh Hunt, 26

"Jenny Kiss'd Me"

Ellery Husted, 24

"I Saw A Maid"

Orrick Johns, 274

"The Door" from *Asphalt and Other Poems*. Reprinted by permission of the author.

Ben Jonson, 5, 29, 30

"The Triumph"; from "The Forest: To Celia"; "Begging Another, on Colour of Mending the Former"

John Keats, 90, 91, 168

"To Fanny"; "Sonnet"; from "Lines to Fanny"

Sidney Keyes, 136, 197

"The Promised Landscape" and "A Hope for Those Separated by War" from *Collected Poems*. Reprinted by permission of Routledge and Kegan Paul Ltd., London.

Henry King, 221

From "The Exequy"

Christopher La Farge, 233

"If I Am but the Water" from *Poems and Portraits*. Copyright, 1940, by Christopher La Farge. Reprinted by permission of Coward-McCann, Inc.

Walter Savage Landor, 212

"Rose Aylmer"

Sidney Lanier, 27

"Evening Song" from *Poems of Sidney Lanier, Edited by His Wife*. Reprinted through the courtesy of Charles Scribner's Sons.

Francis Ledwidge, 10

"Had I a Golden Pound" from *The Complete Poems of Frances Ledwidge*. Reprinted by permission of Coward-McCann, Inc.

Muna Lee, 235

"Melilot" from *Sea Change*. Reprinted by permission of the author.

Richard Lovelace, 111

"Going to the Wars"

Amy Lowell, 216, 255

"Crowned" and "A Decade" from *A Dome of Many-Colored Glass* by Amy Lowell. Copyright, 1912, by Amy Lowell. Reprinted by permission of and arrangement with Houghton Mifflin Company, the authorized publishers.

W. J. Turner, 262

"Tragic Love" from *Songs and Incantations*. Reprinted by permission of J. M. Dent and Sons Ltd.

Pierson Underwood, 107

"Talk Is a Candle" from *Brief Harvest—1940*. Reprinted by permission of the author and the publishers, Katherine and Peter Oliver.

Louis Untermeyer, 277

"The Dark Chamber" from *The Burning Bush* by Louis Untermeyer. Copyright, 1928, by Harcourt, Brace and Company, Inc. Used by permission of the publisher.

Mark Van Doren, 162, 253

"The Whisperer" and "Proper Clay" from *Collected Poems* by Mark Van Doren. Copyright, 1939, by Mark Van Doren. Reprinted by permission of Henry Holt and Company, Inc. and Miss Nannine Joseph.

José Garcia Villa, 39

"There Came You Wishing Me" from *Have Come, Am Here* by José Garcia Villa. Copyright, 1941, 1942, by José Garcia Villa. Reprinted by permission of The Viking Press.

John V. A. Weaver, 213

"Two Ways" from *Collected Poems of John V. A. Weaver*. Copyright, 1926, by Alfred A. Knopf, Inc. Reprinted by permission of the publisher.

Charles Webbe, 119

"Against Indifference"

John Hall Wheelock, 96

"Once In a Lonely Hour" from *The Bright Doom* by John Hall Wheelock. Copyright, 1927, by Charles Scribner's Sons. Used by permission of the publisher.

Laurence Whistler, 174

From "In Time of Suspense." Reprinted by permission of Ann Watkins, Inc. and William Heinemann Ltd.

Walt Whitman, 157, 220

"I Heard You, Solemn Sweet-Pipes of the Organ"; "Sometimes with One I Love"

Anna Wickham, 77

"Song" from *The Contemplative Quarry* by Anna Wickham. Copyright, 1921, by Harcourt, Brace and Company, Inc. Reprinted by permission of the publisher.

William Carlos Williams, 94, 100

"Love Song" and "The Hounded Lovers" from *Selected Poems*. Reprinted by permission of New Directions.

INTRODUCTION

*P*OETRY," said Fontenelle, "is the daughter of love." And Addison remarked in the *Spectator* that "love was the mother of poetry. It makes a footman talk like Oroondates." (Whoever that Eastern potentate may have been!) Whichever you speak of first, the lineage seems established. Certainly love poetry usurps a large domain in all verse! It is also of every kind. It is whimsical, playful, savage, scornful, simple, elaborate, fantastic, or in good earnest. It is airily comic or deeply tragic. The fundamental pangs, appeals, exhortations, and bitter upbraidings are the same in all languages. But although the English-speaking peoples are commonly supposed to be colder of temperament than the Latin or the Oriental, their poetry concerning love, from Chaucer to Donne to Swinburne, proves no such thing. Also the ardor physical is at least equaled by the ardor spiritual in many English poems. If you have the outright speech of Sir Thomas Wyatt in the sixteenth century, you have also the more finely impassioned lyrics and sonnets of both the Brownings in the nineteenth. As to long poems, not only did Alfred, Lord Tennyson make one of his best narratives a monodrama on love, in "Maud," but our own American Edwin Arlington Robinson attained his first wide fame upon the publication of a long poem on the age-old love story of *Tristram*. Name George Meredith as poet and one immediately thinks of his "Love in the Valley."

Nor does love poetry consort only with youth. In his later years Thomas Hardy wrote better love poems than many a younger man. The later love poetry of William Butler Yeats made positive, though not by name, the immortality of Maude Gonne. Though Walter Landor wrote his immortal elegy on Rose Aylmer when just turned thirty, his lyrics to "Ianthe" occupied him from the age of twenty-seven until he was over seventy. He was seventy-one when he published the lines,

> Thou hast not rais'd, Ianthe, such desire
> In any breast as thou hast raised in mine.

And in 1863, twelve years after her death, when Landor was eighty-eight, appeared his famous pronouncement:

> I have since written what no tide
> Shall ever wash away, what men
> Unborn shall read o'er ocean wide
> And find Ianthe's name again.

The Delias, Sylvias, Diaphenias, Chlorises, Phyllises, and Amarillises of three centuries ago, to say nothing of Robert Herrick's famous Julia and Lovelace's Lucasta, recognize across the ages Poe's Helen, Annabel Lee, and Lenore; and Ben Jonson's Celia and the Celia of Witter Bynner. Someone should compile a catalogue of the names the older poets gave their ladies, and of the true names under the disguises— for instance, the Penelope Devereux who inspired Sir Philip Sidney to more than a century of sonnets addressing "Stella." Spenser had, of course, his Amoretti to an Elizabeth whose last name still seems in dispute. Obviously both sonnet cycles lead back to their archetype in the sonnets of Shakespeare. Among modern American women the love sonnets of Edna St. Vincent Millay and of Elinor Wylie recall Elizabeth Barrett Browning's forty-four "Sonnets from the Portuguese," though each writer's style is distinct. Nor is it to be forgotten that Sara Teasdale excelled at the love lyric.

If Scotland be considered a forbidding clime, yet its ballads are highly romantic, and its greatest bard, Robert Burns, is known particularly for his love poetry. As for the Irish, who are not neglected in this selection, Douglas Hyde long ago brought together some beautiful poems in the "Love Songs of Connaught," and the Celt has certainly never been backward in versing love. Thus I have referred rather at random to a mere parcel of the wealth of love poetry in what we call the English tongue. Every good poet, past or present, has paid tribute to Eros, from the anonymous author of "Blow Northerne Wynd!" at the beginning of the fourteenth century down to the modern Walter Benton in *This Is My Beloved*. ⟨The fairly brief lyric and the sonnet seem the chief vehicles of the poetry of love, though longer poems have been mentioned above. This is natural because the expression of love is necessarily a spontaneous and highly emotional matter. Most narrative treatments, from Shakespeare's "Venus and Adonis" on down, involve tragedy with the love story, though there are also the gayer, such as Suckling's "A Ballad upon a Wedding." Love songs, of course, go well with music. The Elizabethan, Thomas Campion, was a masque writer and lutenist, and published magical melodies in his song books. Many modern love lyrics have been given musical settings.

One among many things that may be said for the present volume to which these remarks are introductory, is that it is not, like so many anthologies, a mere reordering of the prior choices of others. Its motivations and arrangement, as explained by the editor, are fresh and valid. It has, naturally, its own interesting peculiarities of choice; but despite the more ambitious projects of poets, it is often in this most intimate of categories—the love poem—that they write their most lasting lines. Nor can that be called strange, if we at all agree with the elder Disraeli when he observed that human love is "the principle of existence and its only end."

WILLIAM ROSE BENÉT

CONTENTS

II DESIRE

III FULFILLMENT

xxvi

V MATURITY

VI LOVE'S IMMORTALITY

EDITOR'S FOREWORD

*T*HERE are all kinds of anthologies. Many are essentially collections without continuity. This one is essentially an integrated sequence. It records the experience of love, in its multiple manifestations, from innocence through passion to remembrance. Its continuity is emotional continuity.

The poems are not arranged chronologically, alphabetically, or by authorship but by the quality of emotion they express, the experience they record. English and American poems of six centuries are grouped to follow the successive stages of love that are the common experience of mankind. Thus the emotion of love is presented not as isolated moments of intense living but as a progression during which, as Traherne said, "the Soul doth by Loving honour and enrich itself," but "above all it does attain itself."

Reminiscence, philosophy, ruminations about love were excluded in selecting the poems. Those that have been chosen are not poems about love but love poems, the direct, personal, and passionate expressions of the poet at whatever stage of love he is when he speaks. The poems are grouped in six main sections under the somewhat arbitrary headings of Innocence, Desire, Fulfillment, Pain and Parting, Maturity, and Love's Immortality. Within each section the tide of emotion ebbs and flows, each poem taking something in thought or imagery from the one before and contributing to the one following.

The first stage—Innocence—contains poems of courtship

and of kissing, of stolen delights and happy dalliance. These are the halcyon days when the God of Love is *a drowsy bumblebee sucking flowers,* and the lover, with eyes undimmed by passion, sees and delights in every facet of his lady's beauty. *Her feet beneath her petticoat,* her dancing *like a wave o' the sea,* even *the liquefaction of her clothes* enchant. And she—*shy as a squirrel and wayward as a swallow*—yet *meddles her to know love and naught can cure it.*

This is *the time of roses. They pluck them as they pass.* The air is magic, *magic as her first breath in the first kiss taken,* mad as his pleading for a *hundred then a thousand kisses more.* These careless lovers do not hear *Time's wingèd chariet hurrying near,* are not afraid of the sting of a honey-drunk bumblebee.

But they are caught. Poems in the next section are poems of lovers hopelessly *entangled in love's snare,* learning the despairs as well as the delights of love. No one now *of all the souls that stand created* except the beloved can set the lover free. His eyes are fixed on his jailer, trying to find the secret of her strange power over him. Now come poems of love's deepest insight and most ardent idealism. Only by proving worthy of it, *true to each other,* steadfast as Keats' *bright star,* can they find the way into the Earthly Paradise. These poems have *infinite passion and the pain of finite hearts that yearn.* They describe the doubts, quarrels, complaints, and reconciliations that have given rise to love poetry always. Matthew Prior in seventeenth-century words describes a quarrel and reconciliation no less graphically than Kenneth Fearing in today's idiom.

The next stage is called Fulfillment, the period of physical and spiritual fulfillment. *Eyes close on doubt and open on desire.* Here are lyrical outbursts of human emotion at high flood, poems of passion, ecstasy, transport. The cautious lover is hedged in *salamanderlike with fire.* The world drops away. Former conceptions of love are forgotten, restraints gone. The jealous one says, *But in my arms till break of day, let the living creature lie, mortal, guilty, but to me, the entirely beautiful.*

There is seldom love without pain, never without parting. Pain and parting have inspired much of our finest love poetry, from tender farewells to bitter reproaches. Here are included the poems of love's frustrations—through disillusionment, death, desertion. Here are the struggles of the heart, still loving, learning to relinquish, to make *the power of the spirit set you beyond the power of the mind to seize you.*

But love often progresses without frustration, though not as many poems are written in love's maturity, to testify to the joy of reaching in love *an age so blest that by its side youth seems to waste instead.* This stage of love has less need to be articulate. In this section several major poets have written special poems to their wives.

The sequence closes with a group of poems affirming the immortality of love. The poets in moments of intense personal loss passionately deny that love ends with death, that an emotion so intense can ever fade from the earth.

The foregoing explains the pattern of this book. The pattern, once determined, automatically influenced the selection of material. Fine love poems had to be reluctantly excluded when they did not fit into the plan. The final selection of particular poems was based on intensity of feeling, sincerity, and brevity and, naturally, on special appeal to the compiler.

Panthers pace in tightest cages, and thunder sounds in smallest rooms.

HELEN HUSTED

I. INNOCENCE

Suffyseth me to love you, Rosémounde,
Thogh ye to me ne do no daliaunce.

—GEOFFREY CHAUCER

THE TRIUMPH

Have you seen but a bright lily grow
   Before rude hands have touch'd it?
Have you marked but the fall of the snow
   Before the soil hath smutch'd it?
Have you felt the wool of beaver,
   Or swan's down ever?
Or have smelt o' the bud o' the brier,
   . Or the nard in the fire?
Or have tasted the bag of the bee?
O so white, O so soft, O so sweet is she!

           —A Celebration of Charis

TO ROSEMOUNDE, A BALLAD

Madame, ye ben of al beaute shryne
As fer as cercled is the mappemounde;
For as the cristal glorious ye shyne,
And lyke ruby ben your chekes rounde.
Therwith ye ben so mery and so jocounde,
That at a revel whan that I see you daunce,
It is an oynement unto my wounde,
Thogh ye to me ne do no daliaunce.

For thogh I wepe of teres ful a tyne,
Yet may that no myn herte nat confounde;
Your seemly voys that ye so smal out-twyne
Maketh my thoght in Joye and blis habounde.
So curteisly I go, with lovë bounde,
That to my-self I say, in my penaunce,
Suffyseth me to love you, Rosémounde,
Thogh ye to me ne do no daliaunce.

Nas never pyke walwed in galauntyne
As I in love am walwed and y-wounde;
For which ful ofte I of myself divyne
That I am trewe Tristram the secounde.
My love may not refreyd be nor afounde,
I brenne ay in an amorous plasaunce.
Do what ye list, I wil your thral be founde,
Thogh ye to me ne do no daliaunce.

THERE IS A LADY SWEET AND KIND

There is a Lady sweet and kind,
Was never face so pleased my mind;
I did but see her passing by,
And yet I love her till I die.

Her gesture, motion, and her smiles,
Her wit, her voice my heart beguiles,
Beguiles my heart, I know not why,
And yet I love her till I die.

Her free behaviour, winning looks,
Will make a lawyer burn his books;
I touched her not, alas! not I,
And yet I love her till I die.

Had I her fast betwixt mine arms,
Judge you that think such sports were harms
Were't any harm? no, no, fie, fie,
For I will love her till I die.

Should I remain confined there
So long as Phoebus in his sphere,
I to request, she to deny,
Yet would I love her till I die.

Cupid is wingèd and doth range,
Her country so my love doth change:
But change she earth, or change she sky,
Yet will I love her till I die.

I'M OWRE YOUNG TO MARRY YET

I am my mammie's ae bairn,
   Wi' unco folk I weary, Sir;
And lying, in a man's bed,
   I'm fley'd wad mak me eerie, Sir.

I'm owre young, I'm owre young,
   I'm owre young to marry yet;
I'm owre young, 'twad be a sin
   To tak me frae my mammie yet.

My mammie coft me a new gown,
    The kirk maun hae the gracing o't;
Were I to lie wi' you, kind Sir,
    I'm feared ye'd spoil the lacing o't...

Hallowmas is come and gane,
    The nights are lang in winter, Sir;
And you an' I in ae bed,
    In truth I dare na venture, Sir...

Fu' loud and shrill the frosty wind
    Blaws throu' the leafless timmer, Sir;
But if ye come this gate again,
    I'll aulder be gin simmer, Sir.

I'm owre young, I'm owre young,
   I'm owre young to marry yet;
I'm owre young, 'twad be a sin
   To tak me frae my mammie yet.

DEAR DARK HEAD

Put your head, darling, darling, darling,
   Your darling black head on my heart above;
Oh, mouth of honey with thyme for fragrance,
   Who, with heart in breast, could deny you love?

Oh, many and many a young girl for me is pining,
   Letting her locks of gold to the cold wind free,
For me, the foremost of our gay young fellows;
   But I'd leave a hundred, pure love, for thee!

Then put your head, darling, darling, darling,
   Your darling black head my heart above;
Oh mouth of honey with thyme for fragrance,
   Who with heart in breast could deny you love?

HAD I A GOLDEN POUND

Had I a golden pound to spend,
My love should mend and sew no more.
And I would buy her a little quern,
Easy to turn on the kitchen floor.

And for her windows curtains white,
With birds in flight and flowers in bloom,
To face with pride the road to town,
And mellow down her sunlit room.

And with silver change we'd prove
The truth of Love to Life's own end,
With hearts the years could but embolden,
Had I a golden pound to spend.

FROM *A BALLAD UPON A WEDDING*

. . . .

... The maid (and thereby hangs a tale)
For such a maid no Whitsun-ale
   Could ever yet produce:
No Grape, that's kindly ripe, could be
So round, so plump, so soft as she,
   Nor half so full of Juice.

Her feet beneath her Petticoat,
Like little mice stole in and out,
   As if they fear'd the light:
But oh! she dances such a way
No Sun upon an Easter day
   Is half so fine a sight.

Her Cheeks so rare a white was on,
No Daisy makes comparison
   (Who sees them is undone)
For streaks of red were mingled there,
Such as are on a Katherine Pear,
   (The side that's next the Sun.)

UPON JULIA'S CLOTHES

When as in silks my Julia goes,
      Then, then (methinks) how sweetly flows
That liquefaction of her clothes.

Next, when I cast mine eyes and see
That brave vibration each way free;
  O how that glittering taketh me!

FROM *LOVE IN THE VALLEY*

Under yonder beech-tree single on the green-sward,
  Couch'd with her arms behind her golden head,
Knees and tresses folded to slip and ripple idly,
  Lies my young love sleeping in the shade.
Had I the heart to slide an arm beneath her,
  Press her parting lips as her waist I gather slow,
Waking in amazement she could not but embrace me:
  Then would she hold me and never let me go?

Shy as the squirrel and wayward as the swallow,
  Swift as the swallow along the river's light
Circleting the surface to meet his mirror'd winglets,
  Fleeter she seems in her stay than in her flight.
Shy as the squirrel that leaps among the pine-tops,
  Wayward as the swallow overhead at set of sun,
She whom I love is hard to catch and conquer;
  Hard, but O the glory of the winning were she won!

When her mother tends her before the laughing mirror,
  Tying up her laces, looping up her hair,
Often she thinks, were this wild thing wedded,
  More love should I have, and much less care.
When her mother tends her before the lighted mirror,
  Loosening her laces, combing down her curls,
Often she thinks, were this wild thing wedded,
  I should miss but one for many boys and girls.

Heartless she is as the shadow in the meadows
  Flying to the hills on a blue and breezy noon.
No, she is athirst and drinking up her wonder:
  Earth to her is young as the slip of the new moon.
Deals she an unkindness, 'tis but her rapid measure,

• *13*

Even as in a dance; and her smile can heal no less:
Like the swinging May-cloud that pelts the flowers with hail-
    stones
Off a sunny border, she was made to bruise and bless.

. . . . . .

Stepping down the hill with her fair companions,
    Arm in arm, all against the raying West,
Boldly she sings to the merry tune she marches,
    Brave in her shape, and sweeter unpossess'd.
Sweeter, for she is what my heart first awaking
    Whisper'd the world was; morning light is she.
Love that so desires would fain keep her changeless;
    Fain would fling the net, and fain have her free.

AD MANUS PUELLAE

For Leonard Smithers

I was always a lover of ladies' hands!
  Or ever mine heart came here to tryst,
For the sake of your carved white hands' commands;
  The tapering fingers, the dainty wrist;
  The hands of a girl were what I kissed.

I remember a hand like a *fleur-de-lys*
  When it slid from its silken sheath, her glove;
With its odours passing ambergris:
  And that was the empty husk of a love.
  Oh, how shall I kiss your hands enough?

They are pale with the pallor of ivories;
  But they blush to the tips like a curled sea-shell:
What treasure, in kingly treasuries,
  Of gold, and spice for the thurible,
  Is sweet as your hands to hoard and tell?

I know not the way from your finger-tips,
  Nor how I shall gain the higher lands,
The citadel of your sacred lips:
  I am captive still of my pleasant bands,
  The hands of a girl, and most, your hands.

O WORLD, BE NOBLER

O World, be nobler, for her sake!
  If she but knew thee what thou art,
What wrongs are borne, what deeds are done
In thee, beneath thy daily sun,
  Know'st thou not that her tender heart
For pain and very shame would break?
O World, be nobler, for her sake!

FROM *INDOLENCE: XII*

Thou didst delight my eyes:
Yet who am I? nor first
Nor last nor best, that durst
Once dream of thee for prize;
Nor this the only time
Thou shalt set love to rhyme.

Thou didst delight my ear:
Ah! little praise; thy voice
Makes other hearts rejoice,
Makes all ears glad that hear;
And short my joy; but yet,
O song, do not forget!

For what wert thou to me?
How shall I say? The moon,
That poured her midnight noon
Upon his wrecking sea;—
A sail that for a day
Has cheered the castaway.

FROM *THE WINTER'S TALE*

Florizel:
  "What you do
Still betters what is done. When you speak, sweet,
I'ld have you do it ever: when you sing,
I'ld have you buy and sell so, so give alms,
Pray so; and for the ordering your affairs,
To sing them too: when you do dance, I wish you
A wave o' the sea, that you might ever do
Nothing but that; move still, still so,
And own no other function: each your doing,
So singular in each particular,
Crowns what you are doing in the present deeds,
That all your acts are queens."

FROM *AMORETTI: III*

What guile is this, that those her golden tresses
She doth attire under a net of gold;
And with sly skill so cunningly them dresses,
That which is gold or hair may scarce be told?
Is it that men's frail eyes, which gaze too bold,
She may entangle in that golden snare;
And being caught, may craftily enfold
Their weaker hearts, which are not well aware?
Take heed therefore, mine eyes, how ye do stare
Henceforth too rashly on that guileful net,
In which if ever ye entrapped are,
Out of her bands ye by no means shall get.
    Folly it were for any being free,
      To covet fetters, though they golden be.

SONG

Nay, but you, who do not love her,
   Is she not pure gold, my mistress?
Holds earth aught—speak truth—above her?
   Aught like this tress, see, and this tress,
And this last fairest tress of all,
So fair, see, ere I let it fall?

Because, you spend your lives in praising;
   To praise, you search the wide world over:
Then, why not witness, calmly gazing,
   If earth holds aught—speak truth—above her?
Above this tress, and this, I touch
But cannot praise, I love so much!

SONG

When Delia on the plain appears,
Aw'd by a thousand tender fears,
I would approach, but dare not move;
Tell me, my heart, if this be love?

Whene'er she speaks, my ravish'd ear
No other voice but her's can hear,
No other wit but her's approve;
Tell me, my heart, if this be love?

If she some other youth commend,
Though I was once his fondest friend,
His instant enemy I prove;
Tell me, my heart, if this be love?

When she is absent, I no more
Delight in all that pleas'd before,
The clearest spring, or shadiest grove;
Tell me, my heart, if this be love?

When fond of pow'r, of beauty vain,
Her nets she spreads for ev'ry swain,
I strove to hate, but vainly strove;
Tell me, my heart, if this be love?

TIME OF ROSES

It was not in the Winter
  Our loving lot was cast,
It was the time of roses—
  We pluck'd them as we passed.

That churlish season never frown'd
  On early lovers yet:
O no—the world was newly crown'd
  With flowers when first we met!

'Twas twilight, and I bade you go,
  But still you held me fast;
It was the time of roses—
  We pluck'd them as we pass'd!

TO A. D.

The nightingale has a lyre of gold,
    The lark's is a clarion call,
And the blackbird plays but a boxwood flute,
    But I love him best of all.

For his song is all of the joy of life,
    And we in the mad, spring weather,
We two have listened till he sang
    Our hearts and lips together.

I SAW A MAID

I saw a maid
With heavy hair,
Moving as light
As wind in air.

Love, you drowsy bumble bee
Sucking flowers,
Don't sting me.

I saw a maid
With gentle eyes
And gentle air
And pillared thighs.

Love, you drowsy bumble bee
Sucking flowers,
Don't sting me.

I saw a maid
With subtle hips
And swelling breasts
And swollen lips.

Love, you drowsy bumble bee
Sucking flowers,
Don't sting me.

I saw a maid
And saw her go
With heavy hair
And motions slow.

Love, you angry bumble bee
Sucking flowers,
You've stung me.

JENNY KISS'D ME

Jenny kiss'd me when we met,
  Jumping from the chair she sat in;
Time, you thief, who love to get
  Sweets into your list, put that in!
Say I'm weary, say I'm sad,
  Say that health and wealth have miss'd me,
Say I'm growing old, but add,
  Jenny kiss'd me.

EVENING SONG

Look off, dear Love, across the sallow sands,
  And mark yon meeting of the sun and sea,
How long they kiss in sight of all the lands.
  Ah! longer, longer, we.

Now in the sea's red vintage melts the sun,
  As Egypt's pearl dissolved in rosy wine,
And Cleopatra night drinks all. 'Tis done,
  Love, lay thine hand in mine.

Come forth, sweet stars, and comfort heaven's heart;
  Glimmer, ye waves, round else unlighted sands.
O night! divorce our sun and sky apart
  Never our lips, our hands.

MEETING AT NIGHT

The grey sea and the long black land;
And the yellow half-moon large and low;
And the startled little waves that leap
In fiery ringlets from their sleep,
As I gain the cove with pushing prow,
And quench its speed in the slushy sand.

Then a mile of warm sea-scented beach;
Three fields to cross till a farm appears;
A tap at the pane, the quick sharp scratch
And blue spurt of a lighted match,
And a voice less loud, thro' its joys and fears,
Than the two hearts beating each to each!

FROM *THE FOREST: TO CELIA*

Kiss me, sweet: the wary lover
Can your favors keep, and cover,
When the common courting jay
All your bounties will betray.
Kiss again: no creature comes.
Kiss, and score up wealthy sums
Upon my lips, thus hardly sundered
While you breathe. First give a hundred.
Then a thousand, then another
Hundred, then unto the other
Add a thousand, and so more:
Till you equal with the store,
All the grass that Rumney yields,
Or the sands in Chelsea fields,
Or the drops in silver Thames,
Or the stars that gild his streams,
In the silent summer-nights,
When youths ply their stol'n delights ...

BEGGING ANOTHER, ON COLOUR
OF MENDING THE FORMER

For Love's sake, kiss me once again!
I long, and should not beg in vain.
Here's none to spy, or see;
Why do you doubt, or stay?
I'll taste as lightly as the bee,
That doth but touch his flower, and flies away.

Once more, and faith, I will be gone—
Can he that loves ask less than one?
Nay, you may err in this,
And all your bounty wrong:
This could be called but half a kiss;
What we're but once to do, we should do long.

I will but mend the last, and tell
Where, how, it would have relished well;
Join lip to lip, and try:
Each suck the other's breath,
And whilst our tongues perplexèd lie,
Let who will think us dead, or wish our death!

THE COY LASS DRESS'D UP IN HER BEST

Do not rumple my Top-Knot,
　　I'll not be kiss'd to Day;
I'll not be hawled and pulled about,
　　Thus on a Holy-day:
Then if your Rudeness you don't leave,
　　No more is to be said:
See this long Pin upon my Sleeve,
　　I'll run up to the Head;
And if you rumple my head Gear,
I'll give you a good flurt on the Ear.

Come upon a Worky-day,
　　When I have my old Clothes on;
I shall not be so nice nor Coy,
　　Nor stand so much upon:
Then hawl, and pull, and do your best,
　　Yet I shall gentle be:
Kiss Hand, and Mouth, and fell my Breast,
　　And tickle to my Knee:
I won't be put out of my rode,
You shall not rumple my Commode.

"SWEET, LET ME GO!"

Sweet, let me go, sweet, let me go!
What do you mean to vex me so?
Cease your pleading force!
Do you think thus to extort remorse?
Now, now! no more! alas, you overbear me,
And I would cry—but some would hear, I fear me.

I KNOW WHERE I'M GOING

I know where I'm going,
And I know who's going with me:
I know who I love,
But the dear knows who I'll marry.

I have stockings of silk,
Shoes of fine green leather,
Combs to buckle my hair
And a ring for every finger.

Some say he's black,
But I say he's bonny,
The fairest of them all,
My handsome winsome Johnny.

Feather beds are soft,
And painted rooms are bonny;
But I would leave them all
To go with my love Johnny.

I know where I'm going,
And I know who's going with me:
I know who I love,
But the dear knows who I'll marry.

SONG

When thy beauty appears
In its graces and airs
All bright as an angel new dropp'd from the sky, '
At distance I gaze and am awed by my fears:
So strangely you dazzle my eye!

But when without art
Your kind thoughts you impart,
When your love runs in blushes through every vein;
When it darts from your eyes, when it pants in your heart,
Then I know you're a woman again.

There's a passion and pride
In our sex (she replied),
And thus, might I gratify both, I would do:
Still an angel appear to each lover beside,
But still be a woman to you.

THERE CAME YOU WISHING ME

There came you wishing me * * *
And so I said * * *
And then you turned your head
With the greatest beauty

Smiting me mercilessly!
And then you said * * *
So that my heart was made
Into the strangest country...

* * * you said, so beauteously,
So that an angel came
To hear that name,
And we caught him tremulously!

COME NOT NEAR MY SONGS

Come not near my songs,
You who are not my lover,
Lest from out that ambush
Leaps my heart upon you!

When my songs are glowing
As an almond thicket
With the bloom upon it,
Lies my heart in ambush
All amid my singing;
Come not near my songs,
You who are not my lover!

Do not hear my songs,
You who are not my lover!
Over-sweet the heart is,
Where my love has bruised it,
Breathe you not that fragrance,
You who are not my lover.
Do not stoop above my song,
With its languor on you,
Lest from out my singing
Leaps my heart upon you!

WHEN I WAS ONE-AND-TWENTY

When I was one-and-twenty
   I heard a wise man say,
"Give crowns, and pounds and guineas
   But not your heart away;
Give pearls away and rubies
   But keep your fancy free."
But I was one-and-twenty,
   No use to talk to me.

When I was one-and-twenty
   I heard him say again,
"The heart out of the bosom
   Was never given in vain;
'Tis paid with sighs a plenty
   And sold for endless rue."
And I am two-and-twenty,
   And oh, 'tis true, 'tis true.

THE LOVER REJOICETH

Tangled was I in Love's snare,
Oppressed with pain, torment with care;
Of grief right sure, of joy full bare,
Clean in despair by cruelty.
But ha! ha! ha! full well is me,
For I am now at liberty.

The woeful days so full of pain,
The weary nights all spent in vain,
The labor lost for so small gain,
To write them all it will not be.
But ha! ha! ha! full well is me,
For I am now at liberty.

With feignéd words which were but wind,
To long delays was I assign'd;
Her wily looks my wits did blind;
Whate'er she would I would agree.
But ha! ha! ha! full well is me,
For I am now at liberty.

Was never bird tangled in lime,
That broke away in better time,
Than I, that rotten boughs did climb,
And had no hurt but 'scapéd free.
Now ha! ha! ha! full well is me,
For I am now at liberty.

MERCILES BEAUTE: III, ESCAPE

Sin I fro Love escaped am so fat,
I never thenk to ben in his prison lene;
Sin I am free, I counte him not a bene.

He may answere, and seye this or that;
I do not fors, I speke right as I mene.
   Sin I fro Love escaped am so fat,
   I never thenk to ben in his prison lene.

Love hath my name ystrike out of his sclat,
And he is strike out of my bokes clene
For ever-mo; ther is non other mene.
   Sin I fro Love escaped am so fat,
   I never thenk to ben in his prison lene;
   Sin I am free, I counte him not a bene.

FREEDOM

Now heaven be thanked, I am out of love again!
I have been long a slave, and now am free;
I have been tortured, and am eased of pain;
I have been blind, and now my eyes can see;
I have been lost, and now my way lies plain;
I have been caged, and now I hold the key;
I have been mad, and now at last am sane;
I am wholly I that was but half of me.
   So a free man, my dull proud path I plod,
    Who, tortured, blind, mad, caged, was once a God.

II. DESIRE

He caught me in his silken net,
And shut me in his golden cage.

—WILLIAM BLAKE

SONG

How sweet I roamed from field to field
    And tasted all the summer's pride,
'Till I the Prince of Love beheld
    Who in the sunny beams did glide!

He showed me lilies for my hair,
    And blushing roses for my brow;
He led me through his gardens fair,
    Where all his golden pleasures grow.

With sweet May dews my wings were wet,
    And Phoebus fired my vocal rage;
He caught me in his silken net,
    And shut me in his golden cage.

He loves to sit and hear me sing,
    Then, laughing, sports and plays with me;
Then stretches out my golden wing,
    And mocks my loss of liberty.

MY TRUE-LOVE HATH MY HEART

My true-love hath my heart, and I have his,
By just exchange one for another given:
I hold his dear, and mine he cannot miss,
There never was a better bargain driven:
    My true-love hath my heart, and I have his.

His heart in me keeps him and me in one,
My heart in him his thoughts and senses guides:
He loves my heart, for once it was his own,
I cherish his because in me it bides:
    My true-love hath my heart, and I have his.

SONNET XII

You're not alone when you are still alone;
O God, from you that I could private be!
Since you one were, I never since was one,
Since you in me, my self since out of me,
Transported from my self into your being,
Though either distant, present yet to either;
Senseless with too much joy, each other seeing,
And only absent when we are together.
Give me my self, and take your self again!
Devise some means but how I may forsake you!
So much is mine that doth with you remain,
That taking what is mine, with me I take you.

    You do bewitch me! O that I could fly
    From my self you, or from your own self I!

SONNET LVII

Being your slave, what should I do but tend
Upon the hours and times of your desire?
I have no precious time at all to spend,
Nor services to do, till you require.
Nor dare I chide the world-without-end hour
Whilst I, my sovereign, watch the clock for you,
Nor think the bitterness of absence sour
When you have bid your servant once adieu;
Nor dare I question with my jealous thought
Where you may be, or your affairs suppose,
But, like a sad slave, stay and think of nought,
Save, where you are, how happy you make those.
  So true a fool is love that in your will,
  Though you do any thing, he thinks no ill.

SONG

Not, Celia, that I juster am
   Or better than the rest;
For I would change each hour like them,
   Were not my heart at rest.

But I am tied to very thee
   By every thought I have:
Thy face I only care to see,
   Thy heart I only crave.

All that in woman is ador'd,
   In thy dear self I find;
For the whole sex can but afford
   The handsome and the kind.

Why then should I seek farther store,
   And still make love anew?
When change itself can give no more,
   'Tis easy to be true.

TO HIS COY MISTRESS

Had we but world enough, and time,
This coyness, Lady, were no crime.
We would sit down, and think which way
To walk and pass our long love's day.
Thou by the Indian Ganges' side
Shouldst rubies find: I by the tide
Of Humber would complain. I would
Love you ten years before the Flood;
And you should, if you please, refuse
Till the conversion of the Jews.
My vegetable love should grow
Vaster than empires, and more slow:
An hundred years should go to praise
Thine eyes and on thy forehead gaze;
Two hundred to adore each breast,
And thirty thousand to the rest;
An age at least to every part,
And the last age should show your heart.
For, Lady, you deserve this state;
Nor would I love at lower rate.

But at my back I always hear
Time's wingéd chariot hurrying near:
And yonder all before us lie
Deserts of vast eternity.
Thy beauty shall no more be found,
Nor, in thy marble vault, shall sound
My echoing song: then worms shall try
That long preserv'd virginity,
And your quaint honour turn to dust,
And into ashes all my lust.

The grave's a fine and private place,
But none, I think, do there embrace.

Now, therefore, while the youthful hue
Sits on thy skin like morning dew,
And while thy willing soul transpires
At every pore with instant fires,
Now let us sport us while we may,
And now, like amorous birds of prey,
Rather at once our Time devour
Than languish in his slow-chapt power.
Let us roll all our strength and all
Our sweetness up into one ball,
And tear our pleasures with rough strife
Through the iron gates of life.
Thus, though we cannot make our sun
Stand still, yet we will make him run.

A SONG OF PRAISE

(For one who praised his lady's being fair.)

You have not heard my love's dark throat,
    Slow-fluting like a reed,
Release the perfect golden note
    She caged there for my need.

Her walk is like the replica
    Of some barbaric dance
Wherein the soul of Africa
    Is winged with arrogance.

And yet so light she steps across
    The ways her sure feet pass,
She does not dent the smoothest moss
    Or bend the thinnest grass.

My love is dark as yours is fair,
    Yet lovelier I hold her
Than listless maids with pallid hair,
    And blood that's thin and colder.

You proud-and-to-be-pitied one,
    Gaze on her and despair;
Then seal your lips until the sun
    Discovers one as fair.

THE HEART'S JOURNEY

IV

What you are I cannot say;
  Only this I know full well—
When I touched your face today
  Drifts of blossom flushed and fell.

Whence you came I cannot tell;
  Only—with your joy you start
Chime on chime from bell on bell
  In the cloisters of my heart.

BE STILL AS YOU ARE BEAUTIFUL

Be still as you are beautiful,
    Be silent as the rose;
     Through miles of starlit countryside
      Unspoken worship flows
To reach you in your loveless room
     From lonely men whom daylight gave
    The blessing of your passing face
      Impenetrably grave.

A white owl in the lichened wood
    Is circling silently;
More secret and more silent yet
   Must be your love to me.
     Thus, while about my dreaming head
    Your soul in ceaseless vigil goes,
Be still as you are beautiful,
    Be silent as the rose.

THE NYMPH'S SONG TO HYLAS

I know a little garden close
Set thick with lily and red rose,
Where I would wander if I might
From dewy dawn to dewy night,
And have one with me wandering.

A RED, RED ROSE

O my Luve is like a red, red rose,
    That's newly sprung in June:
O my Luve is like the melodie
    That's sweetly play'd in tune.

MY LOVE COULD WALK

My Love could walk in richer hues
    Than any bird of paradise,
And no one envy her her dress:
    Since in her looks the world would see
A robin's love and friendliness.

And she could be the lily fair,
    More richly dressed than all her kind,
And no one envy her her gain:
    Since in her looks the world would see
A daisy that was sweet and plain.

Oh, she could sit like any queen
    That's nailed by diamonds to a throne,
Her splendour envied by not one:
    Since in her looks the world would see
A queen that's more than half a nun.

SONG

For her gait, if she be walking;
　　Be she sitting, I desire her
For her state's sake; and admire her
For her wit if she be talking;
　　Gait and state and wit approve her;
　　For which all and each I love her.

Be she sullen, I commend her
For a modest. Be she merry,
For a kind one her prefer I.
Briefly, everything doth lend her
　　So much grace, and so approve her,
　　That for everything I love her.

CHOICE

Of all the souls that stand create
I have elected one,
When sense from spirit files away
And subterfuge is done;

When that which is and that which was
Apart, intrinsic, stand,
And this brief tragedy of flesh
Is shifted like a sand;

When figures show their royal front
And mists are carved away,—
Behold the atom I preferred
To all the lists of clay!

SOMEWHERE I HAVE NEVER TRAVELLED

somewhere i have never travelled, gladly beyond
any experience, your eyes have their silence:
in your most frail gesture are things which enclose me,
or which i cannot touch because they are too near

your slightest look easily will unclose me
though i have closed myself as fingers,
you open always petal by petal myself as Spring opens
(touching skilfully, mysteriously) her first rose

or if your wish be to close me, i and
my life will shut very beautifully, suddenly,
as when the heart of this flower imagines
the snow carefully everywhere descending;

nothing which we are to perceive in this world equals
the power of your intense fragility: whose texture
compels me with the colour of its countries,
rendering death and forever with each breathing

(i do not know what it is about you that closes
and opens; only something in me understands
the voice of your eyes is deeper than all roses)
nobody, not even the rain, has such small hands

FROM *MARPESSA*

... "I love thee then
Not only for thy body packed with sweet
Of all this world, that cup of brimming June,
That jar of violet wine set in the air,
That palest rose sweet in the night of life;
Nor for that stirring bosom all besieged
By drowsing lovers, or thy perilous hair;
Nor for that face that might indeed provoke
Invasion of old cities; no, nor all
Thy freshness stealing on me like strange sleep.
Not for this only do I love thee, but
Because Infinity upon thee broods;
And thou art full of whispers and of shadows.
Thou meanest what the sea has striven to say
So long, and yearnéd up the cliffs to tell;
Thou art what all the winds have uttered not,
What the still night suggesteth to the heart.
Thy voice is like to music heard ere birth,
Some spirit lute touched on a spirit sea;
Thy face remembered is from other worlds,
It has been died for, though I know not when,
It has been sung of, though I know not where.
It has the strangeness of the luring West,
And of sad sea-horizons; beside thee
I am aware of other times and lands,
Of birth far-back, of lives in many stars.
O beauty lone and like a candle clear
In this dark country of the world! Thou art
My woe, my early light, my music dying."

THE INDIAN SERENADE

I arise from dreams of thee
In the first sweet sleep of night,
When the winds are breathing low,
And the stars are shining bright;
I arise from dreams of thee,
And a spirit in my feet
Hath led me—who knows how?
To thy chamber window, Sweet!

The wandering airs they faint
On the dark, the silent stream;
The champak odors fail
Like sweet thoughts in a dream;
The nightingale's complaint,
It dies upon her heart;
As I must die on thine,
Oh, beloved as thou art!

O lift me from the grass!
I die! I faint! I fail!
Let thy love in kisses rain
On my lips and eyelids pale,
My cheek is cold and white, alas!
My heart beats loud and fast;—
Oh! press it to thine own again,
Where it will break at last.

YASMIN

How splendid in the morning glows the lily: with what grace
  he throws
His supplication to the rose: do roses nod the head, Yasmin?

But when the silver dove descends I find the little flower of
  friends
Whose very name that sweetly ends I say when I have said,
  Yasmin.

The morning light is clear and cold: I dare not in that light
  behold
A whiter light, a deeper gold, a glory too far shed, Yasmin.

But when the deep red eye of day is level with the lone
  highway,
And some to Meccah turn to pray, and I toward thy bed,
  Yasmin;

Or when the wind beneath the moon is drifting like a soul
  aswoon,
And harping planets talk love's tune with milky wings
  outspread, Yasmin,

Shower down thy love, O burning bright! For one night or the
  other night
Will come the Gardener in white, and gathered flowers are
  dead, Yasmin.

AN ARAB LOVE-SONG

The hunched camels of the night
Trouble the bright
And silver waters of the moon.
The Maiden of the Morn will soon
Through Heaven stray and sing,
Star-gathering.

Now while the dark about our loves is strewn,
Light of my dark, blood of my heart, O come!
And night will catch her breath up, and be dumb.

Leave thy father, leave thy mother
And thy brother;
Leave the black tents of thy tribe apart!
Am I not thy father and thy brother,
And thy mother?
And thou—what needest with thy tribe's black tents
Who hast the red pavillion of my heart?

I AM IN LOVE WITH HIGH,
FAR-SEEING PLACES

I am in love with high, far-seeing places
That look on plains half-sunlight and half-storm;
In love with hours when from circling faces
Veils pass, and laughing fellowship glows warm.
You who look on me with grave eyes where rapture
And April love of living burn confessed,—
The Gods are good! The world lies free to capture!
Life has no walls. O take me to your breast!
Take me,—be with me for a moment's span!—
I am in love with all unveilèd faces.
I seek the wonder at the heart of man;
I would go up to the far-seeing places.
While youth is ours, turn toward me for a space
The marvel of your rapture-lighted face!

SILENT NOON

Your hands lie open in the long fresh grass,—
The finger-points look through like rosy blooms:
Your eyes smile peace. The pasture gleams and glooms
'Neath billowing skies that scatter and amass.
All round our nest, far as the eye can pass,
Are golden kingcup-fields with silver edge
Where the cow-parsley skirts the hawthorn-hedge.
'Tis visible silence, still as the hour-glass.
Deep in the sun-searched growths the dragon-fly
Hangs like a blue thread loosened from the sky:—
So this winged hour is dropped to us from above.
Oh! clasp we to our hearts, for deathless dower,
This close-companioned inarticulate hour
When twofold silence was the song of love.

SONG OF TROILUS

"If no love is, O God, what fele I so?
And if love is, what thing and whiche is he!
If love be good, from whennes comth my wo?
If it be wikke, a wonder thinketh me,
Whenne every torment and adversitee
That cometh of hym, may to me savory thinke;
For ay thurst I, the more that I it drinke.

And if that at myn owen lust I brenne,
From whennes cometh my wailing and my pleynte?
If harm agree me, where-to pleyne I thenne?
I noot ne why unwery that I feynte.
O quike deth, O swete harm so queynte,
How may of thee in me swich quantitee,
But if that I consente that it be?

And if that I consente, I wrongfully
Compleyne, y-wis; thus possed to and fro,
Al sterelees with-inne a boat am I
A-mid the see, by twixen windes two
That in contrarie stonden ever-mo.
Allas! what is this wonder maladye?
For hete or cold, for cold of hete, I deye."

FROM *ALL FOR LOVE*

HOW I LOVED

Witness, ye days and nights, and all ye hours,
That danced away with down upon your feet,
As all your business were to count my passion!
One day passed by, and nothing saw but love;
Another came, and still 'twas only love:
The suns were wearied out with looking on,
And I untired with loving.
I saw you every day, and all the day;
And every day was still but as the first,
So eager was I still to see you more...

"FOR G"

All night under the moon
Plovers are flying
Over the dreaming meadows of silvery light,
Over the meadows of June
Flying and crying—
Wandering voices of love in the hush of the night.

All night under the moon
Love, though we're lying
Quietly under the thatch, in the silvery light
Over the meadows of June
Together we're flying—
Rapturous voices of love in the hush of the night.

ALL NIGHT LONG

We were in bed by nine, but she did not hear the clock,
She lay in her quiet first sleep, soft-breathing, head by her
    arm,
And the rising radiant moon spilled silver out of its crock,
On her hair and forehead and eyes as we rested, gentle and
    warm.

All night long it remained, that calm, compassionate sheet,
All the night it wrapped us in whiteness like ermine-fur,
I did not sleep all the night, but lay, with wings on my feet,
Still, the cool at my lips, seeing her, worshipping her.

Oh, the bright sparks of dawn when day broke, burning and
    wild!
Oh, the first waking glance from her sleepy, beautiful eyes!
With a heart and a mind newborn as a naked, young, golden
    child,
I took her into my arms. We saw the morning arise!

FROM *THE PRINCESS*

"Now sleeps the crimson petal, now the white;
Nor waves the cypress in the palace walk;
Nor winks the gold fin in the porphyry font:
The fire-fly wakens: waken thou with me.

Now drops the milkwhite peacock like a ghost,
And like a ghost she glimmers on to me.
Now lies the Earth all Danaë to the stars,
And all thy heart lies open unto me.

Now slides the silent meteor on, and leaves
A shining furrow, as thy thoughts in me.

Now folds the lily all her sweetness up,
And slips into the bosom of the lake:
So fold thyself, my dearest, thou, and slip
Into my bosom and be lost in me."

MENTRECHÈ IL VENTO, COME FA, SI TACE

Will you perhaps consent to be
Now that a little while is still
(Ruth of sweet wind) now that a little while
My mind's continuing and unreleasing wind.
Touches this single of your flowers, this one only,
Will you perhaps consent to be
My many-branchéd, small and dearest tree?

My mind's continuing and unreleasing wind
—The wind which is wild and restless, tired and asleep,
The wind which is tired, wild and still continuing,
The wind which is chill, and warm, wet, soft, in every
    influence,
Lusts for Paris, Crete and Pergamus,
Is suddenly off for Paris and Chicago,
Judaea, San Francisco, the Midi,
—May I perhaps return to you
Wet with an Attic dust, and chill from Norway
My dear, so-many-branchéd smallest tree?

Would you perhaps consent to be
The very rack and crucifix of winter, winter's wild
Knife-edged, continuing and unreleasing,
Intent and stripping, ice-caressing wind?
My dear, most dear, so-many-branchéd smallest tree
My mind's continuing and unreleasing wind
Touches this single of your flowers, faith in me,
Wide as the—sky!—accepting as the (air)!
—Consent, consent, consent to be
My many-branchéd, small and dearest tree.

FROM *PARADISE LOST*

She, as a veil down to the slender waist
Her unadorned golden tresses wore
Disheveled, but in wanton ringlets waved
As the vine curls her tendrils, which implied
Subjection, but required with gentle sway,
And by her yielded, by him best received
Yielded with coy submission, modest pride,
And sweet reluctant amorous delay.

DEBT

My debt to you, Belovèd,
 Is one I cannot pay
In any coin of any realm
 On any reckoning day;

For where is he shall figure
 The debt, when all is said,
To one who makes you dream again
 When all the dreams were dead?

Or where is the appraiser
 Who shall the claim compute
Of one who makes you sing again
 When all the songs were mute?

SONG

I was so chill and overworn, and sad,
To be a lady was the only joy I had.
I walked the street as silent as a mouse,
Buying fine clothes, and fittings for the house.

But since I saw my love,
I wear a simple dress,
And happily I move,
Forgetting weariness.

SONNET XXIX

When, in disgrace with Fortune and men's eyes,
I all alone beweep my outcast state,
And trouble deaf heaven with my bootless cries,
And look upon myself, and curse my fate,
Wishing me like to one more rich in hope,
Featured like him, like him with friends possess'd,
Desiring this man's art, and that man's scope,
With what I most enjoy contented least;
Yet in these thoughts myself almost despising,
Haply I think on thee, and then my state,
(Like to the lark at break of day arising)
From sullen earth, sings hymns at Heaven's gate;
   For thy sweet love remember'd such wealth brings
   That then I scorn to change my state with Kings.

ENTRY APRIL 28

Because hate is legislated ... written into
the primer and the testament,
shot into our blood and brain like vaccine or vitamins

Because our day is of time, of hours—and the clock-hand
    turns,
closes the circle upon us: and black timeless night
sucks us in like quicksand, receives us totally—
without a raincheck or a parachute, a key to heaven or the
    last long look

I need love more than ever now .. I need your love,
I need love more than hope or money, wisdom or a drink

Because the slow negative death withers the world—and only
    yes
can turn the tide
Because love has your face and body ... and your hands are
    tender
and your mouth is sweet—and God has made no other eyes
    like yours.

THE GIFT

I thought, belovèd, to have brought to you
A gift of quietness and ease and peace,
Cooling your brow as with the mystic dew
    Dropping from twilight trees.

Homeward I go not yet; the darkness grows;
Not mine the voice to still with peace divine:
From the first fount the stream of quiet flows
    Through other hearts than mine.

Yet of my night I give to you the stars,
And of my sorrow here the sweetest gains,
And, out of hell, beyond its iron bars,
    My scorn of all its pains.

I WOULD FOREGO

I would forego
my snowfields for your sun,
I would surrender
crocus
and ice-gentian
and all the lilies
rising one by one,
one after one,
and then another one
like star that flames white fire
to star
as beacon;

I would forget
the holy marjoram
and all the little speedwells
and low thrift
for just one grain
of your enchantment; lift
the veil,
dividing me from me,
and heal the scar
my searing helmet made,
and lure me forth
radiant,
unafraid
as the immortals;

we near heaven's hills with this,
God's asphodels;
O stay,
stay close,

bend down;
bend down my dream, my Morpheus,
breathe my soul
straight into you;
I would revive the whole
of Ilium
and in sacred trance,
show Helen
who made Troy
a barren town.

ALTER?

Alter? When the hills do.
Falter? When the sun,
Question if his glory
Be the perfect one.

Surfeit? When the daffodil
Doth of the dew:
Even as herself, O friend!
I will of you!

BREAK OF DAY

Stay, O sweet, and do not rise
The light that shines comes from thine eyes;
The day breaks not, it is my heart,
Because that you and I must part.
    Stay, or else my joys will die,
    And perish in their infancy.

'Tis true 'tis day; what though it be?
O, wilt thou therefore rise from me?
Why should we rise because 'tis light?
Did we lie down because 'twas night?
Love which in spite of darkness brought us hither,
Should in despite of light keep us together.

Light hath no tongue, but is all eye;
If it could speak as well as spy,
This were the worst that it could say,
That being well I fain would stay,
And that I lov'd my heart and honour so,
That I would not from him that had them go.

Must business thee from hence remove?
O that's the worst disease of love;
The poor, the foul, the false, love can
Admit, but not the busied man.
He which hath business, and makes love, doth do
Such wrong, as when a married man doth woo.

DO NOT MINUTE

Do not minute
The movements of the soul, for some there are
Of pinion unimpeded, thrice word-swift,
Outsoar the sluggish flesh ... To see and love thee
Was but one soul's step.

THE LOVERS

Willow and water! Would we were
Like those dear lovers all the year,
And our exchanging light and shade
As dark or bright reflection made,
Blending through mirrored rise or fall
And every windless interval.
Might we but touch as tender lipt
As they when first a ripple slipt
To kiss the downward dripping frond
That leaned above the river-pond
To close that envious space between
Lest any weed should intervene,
That beauty over beauty crouched
Might tremble in the thing it touched!
Would love like theirs were ours to live,
So delicate, so sensitive;
But neither sun nor moon shall see
Thy light in mine or mine in thee.

A LINE-STORM SONG

The line-storm clouds fly tattered and swift,
    The road is forlorn all day,
Where a myriad snowy quartz stones lift,
    And the hoof-prints vanish away.
The roadside flowers, too wet for the bee,
    Expend their bloom in vain.
Come over the hills and far with me,
    And be my love in the rain.

The birds have less to say for themselves
    In the wood-world's torn despair
Than now these numberless years the elves,
    Although they are no less there:
All song of the woods is crushed like some
    Wild, easily shattered rose.
Come, be my love in the wet woods, come,
    Where the boughs rain when it blows.

There is the gale to urge behind
    And bruit our singing down,
And the shallow waters aflutter with wind
    From which to gather your gown.
What matter if we go clear to the west,
    And come not through dry-shod?
For wilding brooch shall wet your breast
    The rain-fresh goldenrod.

Oh, never this whelming east wind swells
    But it seems like the sea's return
To the ancient lands where it left the shells
    Before the age of fern;

And it seems like the time when after doubt
　　Our love came back amain.
Oh, come forth into the storm and rout
　　And be my love in the rain.

SONNET

Bright star! would I were steadfast as thou art—
　Not in lone splendour hung aloft the night,
And watching, with eternal lids apart,
　Like Nature's patient, sleepless Eremite,
The moving waters at their priestlike task
　Of pure ablution round earth's human shores,
Or gazing on the new soft fallen mask
　Of snow upon the mountains and the moors—
No—yet still steadfast, still unchangeable,
　Pillow'd upon my fair love's ripening breast,
To feel for ever its soft fall and swell,
　Awake for ever in a sweet unrest;
Still, still to hear her tender-taken breath,
And so live ever—or else swoon to death.

IN A WOMAN'S FACE

Sometimes, in a woman's brow
Beneath the shadow of her hair,
The lover, gazing as I gaze now,
Suddenly finds perfection there;
Sees in her eyes the fire
That burned a city for one man's want,
And made Leander in desire
For Hero swim the Hellespont.

In such a moment, when the eye
Has taken all that flesh can offer,
And closes on satiety,
There comes, as now to me your lover,
A gentleness whose strength
Rebuilds the city that was spoiled.
Then, through the sensual sea, at length,
Two frightened hearts are reconciled.

SONNET: THE TOKEN

Send me some token, that my hope may live
   Or that my ceaseless thoughts may sleep and rest;
Send me some honey to make sweet my hive,
   That in my passion I may hope the best.
I beg no ribbon wrought with thine own hands
   To knit our loves in the fantastic strain
Of new-touch'd youth; nor ring to show the stands
   Of our affection that, as that's round and plain
So should our loves meet in simplicity—
   No, nor the corals, which thy wrist enfold,
Laced up together in congruity,
   To show our thoughts should rest in the same hold;
No, nor thy picture, though most gracious,
   And most desired, because best like the best;
Nor witty lines, which are most copious
   Within the writings which thou hast address'd.

Send me nor this nor that, t' increase my store,
But swear thou think'st I love thee, and no more.

LOVE SONG

What have I to say to you
When we shall meet?
Yet—
I lie here thinking of you.

The stain of love
Is upon the world!
Yellow, yellow, yellow
It eats into the leaves,
Smears with saffron
The horned branches that lean
Heavily
Against a smooth purple sky!

There is no light
Only a honey-thick stain
That drips from leaf to leaf
And limb to limb,
Spoiling the colors
Of the whole world—

I am alone.
The weight of love
Has buoyed me up
Till my head
Knocks against the sky.

See me!
My hair is dripping with nectar—
Starlings carry it
On their black wings.

See, at last
My arms and my hands
Are lying idle.

How can I tell
If I shall ever love you again
As I do now?

ONCE IN A LONELY HOUR

Upon my breast,
   Once in a lonely hour your head was laid,
And you had rest
   From much that troubled you—you were no longer afraid.

But now, even here
   No refuge is; you shall not ever lie
As once, in my heart's shelter here,
   Poor heart, while the great hounds of time go roaring by.

Vain was the strength
   You leaned on, in that hour—you did not guess
How vain the strength
   Whereon you propped your ignorant lovingness.

And yet—what more
   Has life to offer life, here in the lone
Tumult? A little rest, no more—
   Upon a heart as troubled as its own.

SONNET X

From *One Person*

When I perceive the sable of your hair
Silvered, and deep within those caverns are
Your eyesockets, a double-imaged star,
And your fine substance fretted down with care,
Then do I marvel that a woman dare
Prattle of mortal matters near and far
To one so wounded in demonic war
Against some prince of Sirius or Altair.

How is it possible that this hand of clay,
Though white as porcelain, can contrive a touch
So delicate it shall not hurt too much?
What voice can my invention find to say
So soft, precise, and scrupulous a word
You shall not take it for another sword?

THE HILL

Breathless we flung us on the windy hill,
   Laughed in the sun, and kissed the lovely grass.
   You said, "Through glory and ecstasy we pass;
Wind, sun, and earth remain, the birds sing still,
When we are old, are old...." "And when we die
   All's over that is ours; and life burns on
Through other lovers, other lips," said I,
   —"Heart of my heart, our heaven is now, is won!"

"We are Earth's best, that learnt her lesson here.
   Life is our cry. We have kept the faith!" we said;
   "We shall go down with unreluctant tread
Rose-crowned into the darkness!"... Proud we were,
   And laughed, that had such brave true things to say.
   —And then you suddenly cried, and turned away.

OF TEARS

Who would have thought there could have bin
Such joy in tears wept for our sin?
　Mine eyes have seen, my heart hath proved
The most and best of earthly joys:
　The sweets of love, and being loved,
Masks, feasts, and plays, and such like toys.
　Yet this one tear, which now doth fall,
　In true delight exceeds them all.

THE HOUNDED LOVERS

Where shall we go?
Where shall we go
  who are in love?

Juliet went
to Friar Laurence's cell.
  but we have no rest.

Rain water lies
on the hard-packed ground,
  reflecting
  the morning sky,

But where shall we go?
We cannot resolve ourselves
  into a dew

Or sink into the earth.
Shall we postpone it
  to Eternity?

The dry heads
of the goldenrod,
  turned to stiff ghosts,

Jerk at their dead
stalks, signalling hieroglyphs
  of grave warning.

Where shall we go?
The movement of benediction
  does not turn back
  the cold wind.

OH, THE BURDEN, THE BURDEN
OF LOVE UNGIVEN

Oh, the burden, the burden of love ungiven,
  The weight of laughter unshed,
Oh, heavy caresses, unblown tendernesses,
  Oh, love-words unsung and unsaid.

Oh, the burden, the burden of love unspoken,
  The cramp of silence close-furled,
To lips that would utter, to hands that would scatter
  Love's seed on the paths of the world.

Oh, the heavy burden of love ungiven:
  My breast doth this burden bear;
Deep in my bosom the unblown blossom—
  My world-love that withers there.

DOVER BEACH

The sea is calm tonight,
The tide is full, the moon lies fair
Upon the straits;—on the French coast the light
Gleams and is gone; the cliffs of England stand,
Glimmering and vast, out in the tranquil bay.
Come to the window, sweet is the night-air!

Only, from the long line of spray
Where the sea meets the moon-blanched land,
Listen! you hear the grating roar
Of pebbles which the waves draw back, and fling,
At their return, up the high strand,
Begin, and cease, and then again begin,
With tremulous cadence slow, and bring
The eternal note of sadness in.

Sophocles long ago
Heard it on the Aegean, and it brought
Into his mind the turbid ebb and flow
Of human misery; we
Find also in the sound a thought,
Hearing it by this distant northern sea.

The Sea of Faith
Was once, too, at the full, and round earth's shore
Lay like the folds of a bright girdle furled.
But now I only hear
Its melancholy, long, withdrawing roar,

Retreating, to the breath
Of the night-wind, down the vast edges drear
And naked shingles of the world.

Ah, love, let us be true
To one another! for the world, which seems
To lie before us like a land of dreams,
So various, so beautiful, so new,
Hath really neither joy, nor love, nor light,
No certitude, nor peace, nor help for pain;
And we are here as on a darkling plain
Swept with confused alarms of struggle and flight
Where ignorant armies clash by night.

TO CHLOE

Who for his sake wished herself younger.

There are two births; the one when light
　　First strikes the new awaken'd sense;
The other when two souls unite,
　　And we must count our life from thence:
When you loved me and I loved you
Then both of us were born anew.

Love then to us new souls did give
　　And in those souls did plant new powers;
Since when another life we live,
　　The breath we breathe is his, not ours:
Love makes those young whom age doth chill,
And whom he finds young keeps young still.

IN LOVE, IF LOVE BE LOVE

In Love, if Love be Love, if Love be ours,
Faith and unfaith can ne'er be equal powers:
Unfaith in aught is want of faith in all.

It is the little rift within the lute
That by and by will make the music mute,
And ever widening slowly silence all.

The little rift within the lover's lute
Or little pitted speck in garnered fruit,
That rotting inward slowly moulders all.

It is not worth the keeping: let it go:
But shall it? answer, darling, answer, no.
And trust me not at all or all in all.

SPEAK!

Why are thou silent? Is thy love a plant
Of such weak fibre that the treacherous air
Of absence withers what was once so fair?
Is there no debt to pay, no boon to grant?
Yet have my thoughts for thee been vigilant,
Bound to thy service with unceasing care,
The mind's least generous wish a mendicant
For nought but what thy happiness could spare.
Speak!—though this soft warm heart, once free to hold
A thousand tender pleasures, thine and mine,
Be left more desolate, more dreary cold
Than a forsaken bird's-nest filled with snow
'Mid its own bush of leafless eglantine—
Speak, that my torturing doubts their end may know!

TALK IS A CANDLE

Talk is a candle in the dark,
A lantern on a dusty stair.
Speak to me then, that I may mark
And know for sure that you are there.

Talk is a sack of coins to spend,
To roll and jingle on the board.
Unpack your heart, then, gentle friend,
And let me see what gold you hoard.

But do so gently. Thin with time,
Silvered with age, from hand to hand
Words have been passed. Now dull they chime,
And some are false, some contraband.

A Persian in a colored cloak
Ages agone, perchance, this word
Used in an earlier form, in joke,
Bitter, or tender, or absurd

That now I use to tell my love
Something that passes light as air
That yet endures (with stars above)
When neither you nor I are there.

Talk is a candle in the dark.
Speak to me then, and touch my hand,
That on the stair I still may hark
And know you hear and understand.

So sailors listen for the bell
Telling the channel, when at night,
Blind with the fog, they feel the swell
And seek one hidden, shoreward light.

A LETTER

A day was nothing until this; words went
Like horns through traffic, like the instant birds;
A day was dormant, yet-to-be danced among
The sudden neon furniture and books.

It was that intricate familiar thing
When, coughing like the French ambassador,
The postman said his phrase about the rain
And went undeviating through the door.

O, if I wanted legacies, a poem,
An invitation to the dance, or hoped
For declarations of a stranger's love,
My fingers burst like matches on your name.

If it is later now, if the rain has stopped,
If no one dressed in seaweed lurches in
Like some surprised Ophelia with green hands,
I covet reason but for truth like this:

There is communication on the earth
As quiet as the opening of a wing;
There is a wine of choice, and we who drink
Touch all our future to that emphasis.

NEVER SEEK TO TELL THY LOVE

Never seek to tell thy love,
Love that never told can be;
For the gentle wind does move
Silently, invisibly.

I told my love, I told my love,
I told her all my heart,
Trembling, cold, in ghastly fears.
Ah! she did depart!

Soon after she was gone from me,
A traveller came by,
Silently, invisibly:
He took her with a sigh.

IF YOU CAME

If you came to my secret glade,
 Weary with heat,
I would set you down in the shade,
 I would wash your feet.

If you came in the winter sad,
 Wanting for bread,
I would give you the last that I had,
 I would give you my bed.

But the place is hidden apart
 Like a nest by a brook,
And I will not show you my heart
 By a word, by a look.

The place is hidden apart
 Like the nest of a bird:
And I will not show you my heart
 By a look, by a word.

GOING TO THE WARS

(*To Lucasta*)

Tell me not, Sweet, I am unkind,
   That from the nunnery
Of thy chaste breast, and quiet mind,
   To war and arms I fly.

True, a new mistress now I chase,
   The first foe in the field;
And with a stronger faith embrace
   A sword, a horse, a shield.

Yet this inconstancy is such
   As you too shall adore;
I could not love thee, Dear, so much,
   Lov'd I not honour more.

RONDO

Did I love thee? I only did desire
To hold thy body unto mine,
And smite it with strange fire
Of kisses burning as a wine,
And catch thy odorous hair, and twine
It thro' my fingers amorously.
    Did I love thee?

Did I love thee? I only did desire
To watch thine eyelids lilywise
Closed down, and thy warm breath respire
As it came through the thickening sighs,
And speak my love in such fair guise
Of passion's sobbing agony.
    Did I love thee?

Did I love thee? I only did desire
To drink the perfume of thy blood
In vision, and thy senses tire
Seeing them shift from ebb to flood
In consonant sweet interlude,
And if love such a thing not be,
    I loved not thee.

TO A LADY ASKING HIM HOW LONG
HE WOULD LOVE HER

It is not, Celia, in our power
    To say how long our love will last;
It may be we within this hour
    May lose those joys we now do taste;
The Blessèd, that immortal be,
From change in love are only free.

Then since we mortal lovers are,
    Ask not how long our love will last;
But while it does, let us take care
    Each minute be with pleasure past:
Were it not madness to deny
To live because we're sure to die?

"YOU SAY THERE IS NO LOVE"

You say there is no love, my love,
  Unless it lasts for aye!
Oh, folly, there are interludes
  Better than the play.

You say lest it endure, sweet love,
  It is not love for aye?
Oh, blind! Eternity can be
  All in one little day.

FROM *PARADISE LOST*

With thee conversing I forget all time,
All seasons and their change, all please alike.
Sweet is the breath of morn, her rising sweet,
With charm of earliest birds; pleasant the sun,
When first on this delightful land he spreads
His orient beams on herb, tree, fruit, and flower,
Glistering with dew; fragrant the fertile earth
After soft showers; and sweet the coming-on
Of grateful evening mild; then silent night,
With this her solemn bird, and this fair moon,
And these the gems of heaven, her starry train.
But neither breath of morn, when she ascends
With charm of earliest birds; nor rising sun
On this delightful land; nor herb, fruit, flower,
Glistering with dew; nor fragrance after showers;
Nor grateful evening mild, nor silent night,
With this her solemn bird; nor walk by moon,
Or glittering starlight without thee is sweet.

FROM *FAUSTUS*

Was this the face that launched a thousand ships,
And burnt the topless towers of Ilium?
Sweet Helen, make me immortal with a kiss.

Her lips suck forth my soul: see, where it flies!
Come, Helen, come, give me my soul again!
Here will I dwell, for heaven is in these lips,
And all is dross that is not Helena.
I will be Paris, and for love of thee,
Instead of Troy, shall Württemberg be sacked;
And I will combat with weak Menelaus,
And wear thy colors on my plumed crest;
Yea, I will wound Achilles in the heel,
And then return to Helen for a kiss.
O, thou art fairer than the evening air
Clad in the beauty of a thousand stars;
Brighter art thou than flaming Jupiter
When he appeared to hapless Semele;
More lovely than the monarch of the sky
In wanton Arethusa's azured arms;
And none but thou shalt be my paramour.

FROM *SECRET LOVE,*
OR *THE MAIDEN QUEEN*

I feed a flame within, which so torments me
That it both pains my heart, and yet contents me:
'Tis such a pleasing smart, and I so love it,
That I had rather die than once remove it.

Yet he for whom I grieve shall never know it,
My tongue does not betray, nor my eyes shew it.
Not a sigh, not a tear my pain discloses,
But they fall silently like dew on roses.

Thus to prevent my love from being cruel,
My heart's the sacrifice, as 'tis the fuel:
And while I suffer thus to give him quiet,
My faith rewards my love, though he deny it.

On his eyes will I gaze, and there delight me;
While I conceal my love no frown can fright me:
To be more happy I dare not aspire;
Nor can I fall more low, mounting no higher.

FROM *THE SILENT LOVER*

Wrong not, sweet empress of my heart,
    The merit of true passion,
With thinking that he feels no smart,
    That sues for no compassion.

Silence in love bewrays more woe
    Than words, though ne'er so witty:
A beggar that is dumb, you know,
    May challenge double pity.

Then wrong not, dearest to my heart,
    My true, though secret passion;
He smarteth most that hides his smart,
    And sues for no compassion.

AGAINST INDIFFERENCE

More love or more disdain I crave,
Sweet, be not still indifferent:
O send me quickly to my grave,
Or else afford me more content!
Or love or hate me more or less,
For Love abhors all lukewarmness.

Give me a tempest if 'twill drive
Me to the place where I would be;
Or if you'll have me still alive,
Confess you will be kind to me.
Give hopes of bliss or dig my grave:
More love or more disdain I crave.

TO HIS COY LOVE

I pray thee, leave—love me no more,
　　Call home the heart you gave me!
I but in vain that saint adore
　　That can but will not save me.
These poor half-kisses kill me quite—
　　Was ever man thus servèd:
Amidst an ocean of delight
　　For pleasure to be starvèd!

Show me no more those snowy breasts
　　With azure riverets branchèd,
Where, whilst mine eyes with plenty feasts,
　　Yet is my thirst not stanchèd;
O Tantalus, thy pains ne'er tell!
　　By me thou art prevented:
'Tis nothing to be plagued in Hell,
　　But thus in Heaven tormented.

Clip me no more in those dear arms,
　　Nor thy life's comfort call me,
O these are but too powerful charms,
　　And do but more enthrall me!
But see how patient I am grown
　　In all this coil about thee:
Come, nice thing, let my heart alone,
　　I cannot live without thee!

I DO NOT LOVE THEE

I do not love thee!—no! I do not love thee!
And yet when thou art absent I am sad;
   And envy even the bright blue sky above thee,
Whose quiet stars may see thee and be glad.

I do not love thee!—yet, I know not why,
Whate'er thou dost seems still well done, to me:
   And often in my solitude I sigh
That those I do love are not more like thee!

I do not love thee!—yet, when thou art gone,
I hate the sound (though those who speak be near)
   Which breaks the lingering echo of the tone
Thy voice of music leaves upon my ear.

I do not love thee!—yet thy speaking eyes,
With their deep, bright, and most expressive blue,
   Between me and the midnight heaven arise,
Oftener than any eyes I ever knew.

I know I do not love thee! yet, alas!
Others will scarcely trust my candid heart;
   And oft I catch them smiling as they pass,
Because they see me gazing where thou art.

SLEEP, ANGRY BEAUTY

Sleep, angry beauty, sleep and fear not me:
   For who a sleeping lion dares provoke?
It shall suffice me here to sit and see
   Those lips shut up that never kindly spoke.
What sight can more content a lover's mind
Than beauty seeming harmless, if not kind?

My words have charmed her, for secure she sleeps;
   Though guilty much of wrong done to my love;
And in her slumber, see, she close-eyed, weeps!
   Dreams often more than waking passions move.
Plead, Sleep, my cause, and make her soft like thee,
That she in peace may wake and pity me.

MERCURY'S SONG TO PHAEDRA

Fair Iris I love, and hourly I die,
But not for a slip, nor a languishing eye:
She's fickle and false, and there we agree;
For I am as false and as fickle as she:
We neither believe what either can say;
And, neither believing, we neither betray.

'Tis civil to swear, and say things of course;
We mean not the taking for better or worse;
When present, we love, when absent, agree;
I think not of Iris, nor Iris of me:
The legend of love no couple can find
So easy to part, or so equally joined.

LOVE 20¢ THE FIRST QUARTER MILE

All right. I may have lied to you and about you, and made a
few pronouncements a bit too sweeping, perhaps, and
possibly forgotten to tag the bases here or there,
And damned your extravagance, and maligned your tastes,
and libeled your relatives, and slandered a few of your
friends,
O.K.,
Nevertheless, come back.

Come home. I will agree to forget the statements that you
issued so copiously to the neighbors and the press,
And you will forget that figment of your imagination, the
blonde from Detroit;
I will agree that your lady friend who lives above us is not
crazy, bats, nutty as they come, but on the contrary rather
bright,
And you will concede that poor old Steinberg is neither a
drunk, nor a swindler, but simply a guy, on the eccentric
side, trying to get along.
(Are you listening, you bitch, and have you got this straight?)

Because I forgive you, yes, for everything,
I forgive you for being beautiful and generous and wise,
I forgive you, to put it simply, for being alive, and pardon
you, in short, for being you.

Because tonight you are in my hair and eyes,
And every street light that our taxi passes shows me you
again, still you,
And because tonight all other nights are black, all other hours
are cold and far away, and now, this minute, the stars are
very near and bright.

Come back. We will have a celebration to end all celebrations.
We will invite the undertaker who lives beneath us, and a
couple of boys from the office, and some other friends,
And Steinberg, who is off the wagon, by the way, and that
insane woman who lives upstairs, and a few reporters, if
anything should break.

TWO IN AUGUST

Two that could not have lived their single lives
As can some husbands and wives
Did something strange: they tensed their vocal cords
And attacked each other with silences and words
Like catapulted stones and arrowed knives.

Dawn was not yet; night is for loving or sleeping,
Sweet dreams or safe-keeping;
Yet he of the wide brows that were used to laurel
And she, the famed for gentleness, must quarrel,
Furious both of them, and scared, and weeping.

How sleepers groan, twitch, wake to such a mood
Is not well understood,
Nor why two entities grown almost one
Should rend and murder trying to get undone,
With individual tigers in their blood.

In spring's luxuriant weather had the bridal
Transpired, nor had the growing parts been idle,
Nor was it easily dissolved;
Thereafter they tugged but were still intervolved,
With pain prodigious. The exploit was suicidal.

She in terror fled from the marriage chamber
Circuiting the dark room like a string of amber
Round and round and back,
And would not light one lamp against the black,
And heard the clock that clanged: Remember, Remember.

And he must tread barefooted the dim lawn,
Soon he was up and gone;

High in the trees the night-mastered birds were crying
With fear upon their tongues, no singing nor flying
Which are their lovely attitudes by dawn.

Whether those bird-cries were of heaven or hell
There is no way to tell;
In the long ditch of darkness the man walked
Under the hackberry trees where the birds talked
With words too sad and strange to syllable.

PARTING AFTER A QUARREL

You looked at me with eyes grown bright with pain,
    Like some trapped thing's. And then you moved your head
Slowly from side to side, as though the strain
    Ached in your throat with anger and with dread.

And then you turned and left me, and I stood
    With a queer sense of deadness over me,
And only wondered dully that you could
    Fasten your trench-coat up so carefully

Till you were gone. Then all the air was quick
    With my last words, that seemed to leap and quiver.
And in my heart I heard the little click
    Of a door that closes—quietly, forever.

VIRELAY

Thou cruel fair, I go
To seek out any fate but thee,
Since there is none can wound me so,
Nor that has half thy cruelty,
Thou cruel fair, I go.

Forever, then, farewell,
'Tis a long leave I take, but oh!
To tarry with thee here is hell,
And twenty thousand hells to go;
For ever, though, farewell.

THE RECONCILEMENT

Come, let us now resolve at last
    To live and love in quiet;
We'll tie the knot so very fast
    That Time shall ne'er untie it.

The truest joys they seldom prove
    Who free from quarrels live:
'Tis the most tender part of love
    Each other to forgive.

When least I seem'd concern'd, I took
    No pleasure nor no rest;
And when I feign'd an angry look,
    Alas! I loved you best.

Own but the same to me—you'll find
    How blest will be our fate,
O to be happy—to be kind—
    Sure never is too late!

A LOVER'S ANGER

As Cloe came into the room t'other day,
I peevish began: "Where so long could you stay?
In your life-time you never regarded your hour:
You promised at two; and (pray look, child) 'tis four.
A lady's watch needs neither figures nor wheels:
'Tis enough, that 'tis loaded with baubles and seals.
A temper so heedless no mortal can bear—"
Thus far I went on with a resolute air.
"Lord bless me," said she, "Let a body but speak:
Here's an ugly hard rosebud fall'n into my neck:
It has hurt me, and vexed me to such a degree—
See here! for you never believe me; pray see,
On the left side my breast what a mark it has made!"
So saying, her bosom she careless displayed:
That seat of delight I with wonder surveyed,
And forgot every word I designed to have said.

A WOMAN'S LAST WORD

Let's contend no more, Love,
   Strive nor weep;
All be as before, Love,
   —Only sleep!

What so wild as words are?
   I and thou
In debate, as birds are,
   Hawk on bough!

See the creature stalking
   While we speak!
Hush and hide the talking,
   Cheek on cheek!

What so false as truth is,
   False to thee?
Where the serpent's tooth is
   Shun the tree—

Where the apple reddens
   Never pry—
Lest we lose our Edens,
   Eve and I.

Be a god and hold me
   With a charm!
Be a man and fold me
   With thine arm!

Teach me, only teach, Love!
   As I ought
I will speak thy speech, Love,
   Think thy thought—

Meet, if thou require it,
   Both demands,
Laying flesh and spirit
   In thy hands.

That shall be tomorrow
   Not tonight:
I must bury sorrow
   Out of sight:

—Must a little weep, Love,
   (Foolish me!)
And so fall asleep, Love,
   Loved by thee.

WHEN YOU ARE OLD

When you are old and grey and full of sleep,
And nodding by the fire, take down this book,
And slowly read, and dream of the soft look
Your eyes had once, and of their shadows deep;

How many loved your moments of glad grace,
And loved your beauty with love false or true,
But one man loved the pilgrim soul in you,
And loved the sorrows of your changing face;

And bending down beside the glowing bars,
Murmur, a little sadly, how Love fled
And paced upon the mountains overhead
And hid his face amid a crowd of stars.

TO MARGOT HEINEMANN

Heart of the heartless world,
Dear heart, the thought of you
Is the pain at my side,
The shadow that chills my view.

The wind rises in the evening
Reminds that autumn is near.
I am afraid to lose you,
I am afraid of my fear.

On the last mile to Huesca,
The last fence for our pride,
Think so kindly, dear, that I
Sense you at my side.

And if bad luck should lay my strength
Into the shallow grave,
Remember all the good you can;
Don't forget my love.

THE PROMISED LANDSCAPE

For R. J.

How shall I sing for you—
Sharing only
The scared dream of a soldier:
A young man's unbearable
Dream of possession?
How shall I sing for you
With the foul tongue of a soldier?

We march through new mountains
Where crows inhabit
The pitiful cairns.
At morning, the rock-pools
Are matted with ice.
But you are the mountains
And you the journey.

We lie in a ruined farm
Where rats perform
Marvels of balance
Among the rafters.
And rain kisses my lips
Because you are the sky
That bends always over me.

How shall I sing for you
Knowing only
The explorer's sorrow,
The soldier's weariness?
New ranges and rivers
Are never quite revealing
Your promised figure.

How dare I sing for you
I the least worthy
Of lovers you've had:
You the most lovely
Of possible landscapes?

III. FULFILLMENT

Shut out confusion, draw the curtains to
Build the cathedrals of the fire anew.
Close, eyes, on doubt and open on desire.

—LAURENCE WHISTLER

ABSENCE

Western wind, when wilt thou blow,
   The small rain down can rain?
Christ, if my love were in my arms
   And I in my bed again!

FROM *ROMEO AND JULIET*

Jul. Wilt thou be gone? It is not yet near day:
It was the nightingale and not the lark,
That pierced the fearful hollow of thine ear;
Nightly she sings on yond pomegranate-tree.
Believe me, love, it was the nightingale.

Rom.

It was the lark, the herald of the morn,
No nightingale: look, love, what envious streaks
Do lace the severing clouds in yonder east:
Night's candles are burnt out, and jocund day
Stands tiptoe on the misty mountain tops.
I must be gone and live, or stay and die.

Jul.

Yond light is not day-light, I know it, I:
It is some meteor that the sun exhales,
To be to thee this night a torch-bearer,
And light thee on thy way to Mantua:
Therefore stay yet,—thou need'st not to be gone.

Rom.

Let me be ta'en, let me be put to death;
I am content, so thou wilt have it so.
I'll say yon gray is not the morning's eye,
'Tis but the pale reflex of Cynthia's brow;
Nor that is not the lark whose notes do beat
The vaulty heaven so high above our heads:
I have more care to stay than will to go:—
Come, death, and welcome! Juliet wills it so.
How is't, my soul? let's talk; it is not day.

Jul.

It is, it is!—hie hence, be gone, away!
It is the lark that sings so out of tune,
Straining harsh discords and unpleasing sharps.

Some say the lark makes sweet division;
This doth not so, for she divideth us:
Some say the lark and loathed toad change eyes;
O, now I would they had changed voices too!
Since arm from arm that voice doth us affray,
Hunting thee hence with hunt's-up to the day.
O, now be gone; more light and light it grows.

Rom.

More light and light—more dark and dark our woes!

SECRECY PROTESTED

Fear not (dear Love) that I'll reveal
Those hours of pleasure we two steal;
No eye shall see, nor yet the Sun
Descry what thou and I have done;

No ear shall hear our love, but we
Silent as the night will be;
The god of love himself (whose dart
Did first wound mine and then thy heart),

Shall never know, that we can tell,
What sweets in stoln embraces dwell.
This only meanes may find it out,
If, when I die, physicians doubt

What caus'd my death, and there to view
Of all their judgments which was true—
Rip up my heart, oh! then, I fear,
The world will see thy picture there.

PRELUDE I

When first we met, our souls stood up,
Our garments fell away;
We quite forgot to drink or sup,
We had so much to say.
But no one seemed to be aware
That I had risen from my chair,
And no one saw you bold and bare,
Yet naked at the feast we stood,
And all was beautiful and good.

When we came back through fiery mist,
I touched my gown at throat and wrist,
Surprised to find it still was there,
But none had seen us come and go,
And where we went I do not know,
Or if we walked on dew or snow,
Or if we smelled of flowers or flame—
But nothing since has been the same!

THE GOOD-MORROW

I wonder, by my troth, what thou and I
Did, till we lov'd? were we not wean'd till then?
But sucked on country pleasures, childishly?
Or snorted we in the Seven Sleepers' den?
'Twas so; but this, all pleasures fancies be.
If ever any beauty I did see,
Which I desir'd, and got, 'twas but a dream of thee.

And now good morrow to our waking souls,
Which watch not one another out of fear;
For love all love of other sights controls,
And makes one little room an everywhere.
Let sea-discoverers to new worlds have gone;
Let maps to other, worlds on worlds have shown,
Let us possess one world: each hath one, and is one.

My face in thine eye, thine in mine appears,
And true plain hearts do in the faces rest;
Where can we find two better hemispheres,
Without sharp North, without declining West?
Whatever dies, was not mix'd equally;
If our two loves be one, or thou and I
Love so alike that none do slacken, none can die.

Behold, thou art fair, my love; behold, thou art fair; thou hast doves' eyes within thy locks: thy hair is as a flock of goats that appear from mount Gilead.

Thy teeth are like a flock of sheep that are even shorn, which came up from the washing; whereof every one bear twins, and none is barren among them.

Thy lips are like a thread of scarlet, and thy speech is comely; thy temples are like a piece of a pomegranate within thy locks;

Thy neck is like the tower of David builded for an armoury, whereon there hang a thousand bucklers, all shields of mighty men.

Thy two breasts are like two young roes that are twins, which feed among the lilies.

Until the day break, and the shadows flee away, I will get me to the mountain of myrrh, and to the hill of frankincense.

Thou art all fair, my love; there is no spot in thee.

Come with me from Lebanon, my spouse, with me from Lebanon: look from the top of Amana, from the top of Shenir and Hermon, from the lions' dens, from the mountains of the leopards.

Thou hast ravished my heart, my sister, my spouse; thou hast ravished my heart with one of thine eyes, with one chain of thy neck.

How fair is thy love, my sister, my spouse! how much better is thy love than wine! and the smell of thine ointments than all spices!

Thy lips, O my spouse, drop as the honeycomb: honey and milk are under thy tongue; and the smell of thy garments is like the smell of Lebanon.

A garden inclosed is my sister, my spouse; a spring shut up, a fountain sealed.

Thy plants are an orchard of pomegranates, with pleasant fruits; camphire, with spikenard,

Spikenard and saffron; calamus and cinnamon, with all trees of frankincense; myrrh and aloes, with all the chief spices:

A fountain of gardens, a well of living waters, and streams from Lebanon.

Awake, O north wind; and come, thou south; blow upon my garden, that the spices thereof may flow out. Let my beloved come into his garden, and eat his pleasant fruits.

I am come into my garden, my sister, my spouse: I have gathered my myrrh with my spice; I have eaten my honey-comb with my honey; I have drunk my wine with my milk: eat, O friends; drink, yea, drink abundantly, O beloved.

I sleep, but my heart waketh: it is the voice of my beloved that knocketh, saying, Open to me, my sister, my love, my dove, my undefiled: for my head is filled with dew, and my locks with the drops of the night.

I have put off my coat; how shall I put it on? I have washed my feet; how shall I defile them?

My beloved put in his hand by the hole of the door, and my bowels were moved for him.

I rose up to open to my beloved; and my hands dropped with myrrh, and my fingers with sweet smelling myrrh, upon the handles of the lock.

I opened to my beloved; but my beloved had withdrawn himself, and was gone: my soul failed when he spake: I sought him, but I could not find him; I called him, but he gave me no answer.

The watchmen that went about the city found me, they smote me, they wounded me; the keepers of the walls took away my veil from me.

I charge you, O daughters of Jerusalem, if ye find my beloved, that ye tell him, that I am sick of love.

What is thy beloved more than another beloved, O thou fairest among women? what is thy beloved more than another beloved, that thou dost so charge us?

My beloved is white and ruddy, the chiefest among ten thousand.

His head is as the most fine gold; his locks are bushy, and black as a raven;

His eyes are as the eyes of doves by the rivers of waters, washed with milk, and fitly set.

His cheeks are as a bed of spices, as sweet flowers; his lips like lilies, dropping sweet-smelling myrrh.

His hands are as gold rings set with the beryl; his belly is as bright ivory overlaid with sapphires;

His legs are as pillars of marble, set upon sockets of fine gold; his countenance is as Lebanon, excellent as the cedars;

His mouth is most sweet: yea, he is altogether lovely. This is my beloved, and this is my friend, O daughters of Jerusalem.

How beautiful are thy feet with shoes, O prince's daughter! the joints of thy thighs are like jewels, the work of the hands of a cunning workman.

Thy navel is like a round goblet, which wanteth not liquor; thy belly is like an heap of wheat set about with lilies;

Thy two breasts are like two young roes that are twins;

Thy neck is as a tower of ivory; thine eyes like the fishpools in Heshbon, by the gates of Bathrabbim; thy nose is as the tower of Lebanon which looketh toward Damascus;

Thine head upon thee is like Carmel, and the hair of thine head like purple—the king is held in the galleries.

How fair and how pleasant art thou, O love, for delights!

This thy stature is like to a palm tree, and thy breasts to clusters of grapes.

I said, I will go up to the palm tree, I will take hold of the boughs thereof. Now also thy breasts shall be as clusters of the vine; and the smell of thy nose like apples;

And the roof of thy mouth like the best wine for my beloved, that goeth down sweetly, causing the lips of those that are asleep to speak.

I am my beloved's, and his desire is toward me.

Come, my beloved, let us go forth into the field; let us lodge in the villages;

Let us get up early to the vineyards; let us see if the vine flourish, whether the tender grape appear, and the pomegranates bud forth. There will I give thee my loves.

The mandrakes give a smell, and at our gates are all manner of pleasant fruits, new and old, which I have laid up for thee, O my beloved.

PSALM TO MY BELOVÈD

Lo, I have opened unto you the wide gates of my being,
And like a tide you have flowed into me.
The innermost recesses of my spirit are full of you,
    and all the channels of my soul are grown sweet
    with your presence.
For you have brought me peace;
The peace of great tranquil waters, and the quiet of the
    summer sea.
Your hands are filled with peace as the noon-tide is filled with
    light; about your head is bound the eternal quiet of the
    stars, and in your heart dwells the calm miracle of twi-
    light.
I am utterly content.
In all my spirit is no ripple of unrest,
For I have opened unto you the wide gates of my being
And like a tide you have flowed into me.

THE HEART OF THE WOMAN

O what to me the little room
That was brimmed up with prayer and rest;
He bade me out into the gloom
And my breast lies on his breast.

O what to me my mother's care,
The house where I was safe and warm;
The shadowy blossom of my hair
Will hide us from the bitter storm.

O hiding hair and dewy eyes,
I am no more with life or death,
My heart upon his warm heart lies,
My breath is mixed into his breath.

WILD NIGHTS!

Wild nights! Wild nights!
Were I with thee,
Wild nights should be
Our luxury!

Futile the winds
To a heart in port,—
Done with the compass,
Done with the chart.

Rowing in Eden.
Ah! the sea!
Might I but moor
Tonight in thee!

IT WAS A QUIET WAY

It was a quiet way
He asked if I was his.
I made no answer of the tongue
But answer of the eyes.

And then he bore me high
Before this mortal noise,
With swiftness as of chariots
And distance as of wheels.

The world did drop away
As countries from the feet
Of him that leaneth in balloon
Upon an ether street.

The gulf behind was not—
The continents were new.
Eternity it was—before
Eternity was due.

No seasons were to us—
It was not night nor noon,
For sunrise stopped upon the place
And fastened it in dawn.

BRIDAL SONG

Hold back thy hours, dark Night, till we have done;
    The Day will come too soon.
Young maids will curse thee, if thou steal'st away
And leav'st their losses open to the day.
    Stay, stay, and hide
    The blushes of the bride.

Stay, gentle Night, and with thy darkness cover
    The kisses of her lover.
Stay, and confound her tears and her shrill cryings,
Her weak denials, vows, and often-dyings;
    Stay, and hide all:
    But help not, though she call.

I HEARD YOU, SOLEMN-SWEET PIPES
OF THE ORGAN

I heard you, solemn-sweet pipes of the organ as last Sunday
  morn I pass'd the church,
Winds of autumn, as I walk'd the woods at dusk I heard your
  long stretch'd sighs up above so mournful,
I heard the perfect Italian tenor singing at the opera, I heard
  the soprano in the midst of the quartet singing;
Heart of my love! you too I heard murmuring low through
  one of the wrists around my head,
Heard the pulse of you when all was still, ringing little bells
  last night under my ear.

AND LOVE HUNG STILL

And love hung still as crystal over the bed
   And filled the corners of the enormous room;
The boom of dawn that left her sleeping, showing
   The flowers mirrored in the mahogany table.

O my love, if only I were able
   To protract this hour of quiet after passion,
Not ration happiness but keep this door for ever
   Closed on the world, its own world closed within it.

But dawn's waves trouble with the bubbling minute,
   The names of books come clear upon their shelves,
The reason delves for duty and you will wake
   With a start and go on living on your own.

The first train passes and the windows groan,
   Voices will hector and your voice become
A drum in tune with theirs, which all last night
   Like sap that fingered through a hungry tree
Asserted our one night's identity.

FROM *LAMENT OF AHANIA*

Where is my golden palace?
Where my ivory bed?
Where the joy of my morning hour?
Where the Sons of Eternity singing,

To awaken bright Urizen, my King
To arise to the morning sport,
To the bliss of eternal valleys;

To awake my King in the morn.
To embrace Ahania's joy
On the breadth of his open bosom,
From my soft cloud of dew to fall
In showers of life on his harvests?

When he gave my happy soul
To the Sons of Eternal Joy,
When he took the Daughters of Life
Into my chambers of love.

CLOTHES DO BUT CHEAT AND COZEN US

Away with silks, away with lawn,
I'll have no scenes or curtains drawn;
Give me my mistress as she is,
Dress'd in her nak't simplicities:
For as my heart, e'en so my eye
Is won with flesh, not drapery.

IF THOU LONGEST SO MUCH TO LEARN

If thou longest so much to learn, sweet boy, what 'tis to love,
Do but fix thy thoughts on me and thou shalt quickly prove.
   Little suit, at first, shall win
     Way to thy abashed desire,
   But then will I hedge thee in,
Salamander-like with fire!

THE WHISPERER

Be extra careful by this door,
No least, least sound, she said.
It is my brother Oliver's,
And he would strike you dead.

Come on. It is the top step now,
And carpet all the way.
But wide enough for only one,
Unless you carry me.

I love your face as hot as this.
Put me down, though, and creep.
My father! He would strangle you,
I think, like any sheep.

Now take me up again, again:
We're at the landing post.
You hear her saying Hush, and Hush?
It is my mother's ghost.

She would have loved you, loving me.
She had a voice as fine—
I love you more for such a kiss,
And here is mine, is mine.

And one for her—Oh, quick, the door!
I cannot bear it so.
The vestibule, and out; for now
Who passes that would know?

Here we could stand all night and let
Strange people smile and stare.
But you must go, and I must lie
Alone up there, up there.

Remember? But I understand.
More with a kiss is said.
And do not mind it if I cry,
Passing my mother's bed.

FROM *"ONE PERSON"*

I hereby swear that to uphold your house
I would lay my bones in quick destroying lime
Or turn my flesh to timber for all time;
Cut down my womanhood; lop off the boughs
Of that perpetual ecstasy that grows
From the heart's core; condemn it as a crime
If it be broader than a beam, or climb
Above the stature that your roof allows.

I am not the hearthstone nor the cornerstone
Within this noble fabric you have builded;
Not by my beauty was its cornice gilded;
Not on my courage were its arches thrown:
My lord, adjudge my strength, and set me where
I bear a little more than I can bear.

LAY YOUR SLEEPING HEAD

Lay your sleeping head, my love,
Human on my faithless arm;
Time and fevers burn away
Individual beauty from
Thoughtful children, and the grave
Proves the child ephemeral:
But in my arms till break of day
Let the living creature lie,
Mortal, guilty, but to me
The entirely beautiful.

Soul and body have no bounds:
To lovers as they lie upon
Her tolerant enchanted slope
In their ordinary swoon,
Grave the vision Venus sends
Of supernatural sympathy,
Universal love and hope;
While an abstract insight wakes
Among the glaciers and the rocks
The hermit's sensual ecstasy.

Certainty, fidelity
On the stroke of midnight pass
Like vibrations of a bell,
And fashionable madmen raise
Their pedantic boring cry:
Every farthing of the cost,
All the dreaded cards foretell,
Shall be paid, but from this night
Not a whisper, not a thought,
Not a kiss nor look be lost.

Beauty, midnight, vision dies:
Let the winds of dawn that blow
Softly round your dreaming head
Such a day of sweetness show
Eye and knocking heart may bless,
Find the mortal world enough;
Noons of dryness see you fed
By the involuntary powers,
Nights of insult let you pass
Watched by every human love.

FROM *HESPERIA*

The delight of thy face, and the sound of thy feet, and the
wind of thy tresses,
And all of a man that regrets, and all of a maid that allures.
But thy bosom is warm for my face and profound as a
manifold flower,
Thy silence as music, thy voice as an odor that fades in a
flame;
Not a dream, not a dream is the kiss of thy mouth and the
bountiful hour
That makes me forget what was sin, and would make me
forget were it shame.

FROM *LINES TO FANNY*

O, for some sunny spell
To dissipate the shadows of this hell!
Say they are gone,—with the new dawning light
Steps forth my lady bright!
O, let me once more rest
My soul upon that dazzling breast!
Let once again these aching arms be plac'd,
The tender gaolers of thy waist!
And let me feel that warm breath here and there
To spread a rapture in my very hair,—
O, the sweetness of the pain!
Give me those lips again!
Enough! enough! it is enough for me
To dream of thee!

EVADNE

I first tasted under Apollo's lips
love and love sweetness,
I Evadne;
my hair is made of crisp violets
or hyacinth which the wind combs back
across some rock shelf;
I Evadne
was mate of the god of light.

His hair was crisp to my mouth
as the flower of the crocus,
across my cheek,
cool as the silver cress
on Erotos bank;
between my chin and throat
his mouth slipped over and over.

Still between my arm and shoulder,
I feel the brush of his hair,
and my hands keep the gold they took
as they wandered over and over
that great arm-full of yellow flowers.

DAWN

So begins the day,
Solid, chill, and gray,
But my heart will wake
Happy for your sake;
No more tossed and wild,
Singing like a child,
Quiet as a flower
In this first gray hour.

So my heart will wake
Happy, for your sake.

COMPLETION

My heart has fed today.
My heart, like hind at play,
Has grazed in fields of love, and washed in streams
Of quick imperishable dreams.

In moth-white beauty shimmering,
Lovely as birches in the moon glimmering,
From coigns of sleep my eyes
Saw dawn and love arise.

And like a bird at rest,
Steady in a swinging nest,
My heart at peace lay gloriously
While wings of ecstasy
Beat round me and above.

I am fulfilled of love.

THE VISITING SEA

As the inhastening tide doth roll,
Home from the deep, along the whole
    Wide shining strand, and floods the caves
    —Your love comes filling with happy waves
The open sea-shore of my soul.

But inland from the seaward spaces,
None knows, not even you, the places
    Brimmed, at your coming, out of sight,
    —The little solitudes of delight
This tide constrains in dim embraces.

You see the happy shore, wave-rimmed,
But know not of the quiet dimmed
    Rivers your coming floods and fills,
    The little pools 'mid happier hills,
My silent rivulets, over-brimmed.

What, I have secrets from you ? Yes.
But, visiting Sea, your love doth press
    And reach in further than you know,
    And fills all these; and, when you go,
There's loneliness in loneliness.

A BIRTHDAY

My heart is like a singing bird
   Whose nest is in a watered shoot;
My heart is like an apple-tree
   Whose boughs are bent with thick-set fruit;
My heart is like a rainbow shell
   That paddles in a halcyon sea;
My heart is gladder than all these
   Because my love is come to me.

Raise me a dais of silk and down;
   Hang it with vair and purple dyes;
Carve it in doves, and pomegranates,
   And peacocks with a hundred eyes;
Work it in gold and silver grapes,
   In leaves and silver fleurs-de-lys;
Because the birthday of my life
   Is come, my love is come to me.

FROM *IN TIME OF SUSPENSE*

. . . . . .

Draw-to the curtains then, and let it rain.
We'll look no more on that disordered scene:
Blind rage upon a blinded window-pane,
The shivering white upon the darkening green;
Nor that beyond it leaping to and fro,
Ghost in the ruined garden, or mad briar.
Shut out confusion, draw the curtains to,
Build the cathedrals of the fire anew.
Close, eyes, on doubt and open on desire.

Here, in the quiet brilliance of belief
We fashion life at such intensity,
The very chairs might rustle into leaf
And panels grope to build their primal tree.
Now when our bodies meet like star and star,
Now when our minds remoter commerce do,
No wish too subtle and no world too far,
But we, so perfectly in tune we are,
Passionately conceive and make it true.

SUDDEN LIGHT

I have been here before,
    But when or how I cannot tell:
I know the grass beyond the door,
    The sweet keen smell,
The sighing sound, the lights around the shore.

You have been mine before,—
    How long ago I may not know:
But just when at that swallow's soar
    Your neck turned so,
Some veil did fall,—I knew it all of yore.

Has this been thus before?
    And shall not thus time's eddying flight
Still with our lives our loves restore
    In death's despite.
And day and night yield one delight once more?

DEBT

What do I owe to you
　　Who loved me deep and long?
You never gave my spirit wings
　　Or gave my heart a song.

But oh, to him I loved
　　Who loved me not at all,
I owe the little gate
　　That led through heaven's wall.

FROM *SONNETS FROM THE PORTUGUESE*

When our two souls stand up erect and strong,
Face to face, silent, drawing nigh and nigher,
Until the lengthening wings break into fire
At either curvèd point,—what bitter wrong
Can the earth do to us, that we should not long
Be here contented? Think. In mounting higher,
The angels would press on us and aspire
To drop some golden orb of perfect song
Into our deep, dear silence. Let us stay
Rather on earth, Belovèd,—where the unfit
Contrarious moods of men recoil away
And isolate pure spirits, and permit
A place to stand and love in for a day,
With darkness and the death-hour rounding it.

FROM *LIFE AND DEATH OF JASON—BOOK IX*

... "Upon the day thou weariest of me,
I wish thou mayest somewhat think of this,
And 'twixt thy new-found kisses, and the bliss
Of something sweeter than thy old delight,
Remember thee a little of this night
Of marvels, and this starlit, silent place,
And these two lovers standing face to face."

"O love," he said, "by what things shall I swear
That while I live thou shalt not be less dear
Than thou art now?"
        "Nay, sweet," she said, "let be;
Wert thou more fickle than the restless sea,
Still would I love thee, knowing thee for such;
Whom I know not, indeed, but fear the touch,
Of Fortune's hands when she beholds our bliss,
And knows that nought is good to me but this."

SONG

Sweetest love, I do not go,
  For weariness of thee,
Nor in hope the world can show
  A fitter love for me;
    But since that I
Must die at last, 'tis best,
To use myself in jest
  Thus by feign'd deaths to die;

Yesternight the Sun went hence,
  And yet is here today;
He hath no desire nor sense,
  Nor half so short a way.
    Then fear not me,
But believe that I shall make
Speedier journeys, since I take
  More wings and spurs than he.

O how feeble is man's power,
  That if good fortune fall,
Cannot add another hour,
  Nor a lost hour recall!
    But come bad chance,
And we join to it our strength,
And we teach it art and length,
  Itself o'er us t'advance.

When thou sigh'st, thou sigh'st not wind,
  But sigh'st my soul away;
When thou weep'st, unkindly kind,
  My life's blood doth decay.

It cannot be
That thou lov'st me as thou say'st,
If in thine my life thou waste,
    Thou art the best of me.

Let not thy divining heart
    Forethink me any ill;
Destiny may take thy part,
    And may thy fears fulfil;
        But think that we
Are but turn'd aside to sleep.
They who one another keep
    Alive, ne'er parted be.

ENTRY NOVEMBER 12

I waited years today ... one year for every hour,
all day—though I knew you could not come till night
I waited ... and nothing else in this God's hell meant anything.

I had everything you love—shellfish and saltsticks ... water-
      cress,
black olives. Wine (for the watch I pawned), real cream
for our coffee. Smoked cheese, currants in port, preserved wild
      cherries.

I bought purple asters from a pushcart florist and placed
      them where
they would be between us—
imagining your lovely face among them ...

But you did not come ... you did not come.
You did not come. And I left the table lit and your glass
      filled—
and my glass empty ... and I went into the night, looking
      for you.

The glittering pile, Manhattan, swarmed like an uncovered
      dung heap.
Along the waterfront
manlike shapes all shoulders and collar walked stiffly like
      shadow figures.

Later, the half-moon rose.
                  Everywhere the windows falling dark.
By St. Mark's church, under the iron fence, a girl was crying.
      And the old
steeple was mouldy with moonlight, and I was tired ... and
      very lonely.

THE MEETING

We started speaking,
Looked at each other, then turned away.
The tears kept rising to my eyes
But I could not weep.
I wanted to take your hand
But my hand trembled.
You kept counting the days
Before we should meet again.
But both of us felt in our hearts
That we parted for ever and ever.
    The ticking of the little clock filled the quiet room.
"Listen," I said. "It is so loud,
Like a horse galloping on a lonely road,
As loud as that—a horse galloping past in the night."

    You shut me up in your arms.
But the sound of the clock stifled our hearts' beating.
You said, "I cannot go: all that is living of me
Is here for ever and ever."
Then you went.
    The world changed. The sound of the clock grew fainter,
Dwindled away, became a minute thing.
I whispered in the darkness, "If it stops, I shall die."

ABSENT YET PRESENT

As the flight of a river
That flows to the sea
My soul rushes ever
In tumult to thee.

A twofold existence
I am where thou art;
My heart in the distance
Beats close to thy heart.

Look up, I am near thee,
I gaze on thy face;
I see thee, I hear thee,
I feel thine embrace. . . .

But all that I care for,
And all that I know,
Is that, without wherefore,
I worship thee so. . . .

A twofold existence
I am where thou art;
Hark, hear in the distance
The beat of my heart!

SONNET XCVII

How like a winter hath my absence been
From thee, the pleasure of the fleeting year!
What freezings have I felt, what dark days seen!
What old December's bareness every where!
And yet this time removed was summer's time,
The teeming autumn, big with rich increase,
Bearing the wanton burthen of the prime,
Like widowed wombs after their lords' decease:
Yet this abundant issue seem'd to me
But hope of orphans and unfather'd fruit;
For summer and his pleasures wait on thee,
And, thou away, the very birds are mute;
   Or, if they sing, 'tis with so dull a cheer,
   That leaves look pale, dreading the winter's near.

IV. PAIN AND PARTING

So, we'll go no more a-roving
  So late into the night,
Though the heart be still as loving,
  And the moon be still as bright.

— GEORGE GORDON, LORD BYRON

THE PARTING

Since there's no help, come let us kiss and part—
Nay, I have done, you get no more of me;
And I am glad, yea, glad with all my heart,
That thus so cleanly I myself can free.
Shake hands forever, cancel all our vows,
And, when we meet at any time again,
Be it not seen in either of our brows
That we one jot of former love retain.
Now at the last gasp of Love's latest breath,
When, his pulse failing, Passion speechless lies,
When Faith is kneeling by his bed of death,
And Innocence is closing up his eyes,
—Now if thou wouldst, when all have given him over,
From death to life thou might'st him yet recover.

FROM *ANTONY AND CLEOPATRA*

Give me my robe, put on my crown; I have
Immortal longings in me: now no more
The juice of Egypt's grape shall moist this lip:—
Yare, yare, good Iras; quick. Methinks I hear
Antony call; I see him rouse himself
To praise my noble act; I hear him mock
The luck of Caesar, which the gods give men
To excuse their after wrath:—husband, I come:
Now to that name my courage prove my title!
I am fire and air; my other elements
I give to baser life.—So—have you done?
Come then, and take the last warmth of my lips.
Farewell, kind Charmian. Iras, long farewell.
Have I the aspic in my lips? Dost fall?
If thou and nature can so gently part,
The stroke of death is as a lover's pinch,
Which hurts, and is desired. Dost thou lie still?
If thus thou vanishest, thou tell'st the world
It is not worth leave-taking.

WE'LL GO NO MORE A-ROVING

So, we'll go no more a-roving
   So late into the night,
Though the heart be still as loving,
   And the moon be still as bright.

For the sword outwears its sheath,
   And the soul wears out the breast,
And the heart must pause to breathe,
   And love itself have rest.

Though the night was made for loving,
   And the day returns too soon,
Yet we'll go no more a-roving
   By the light of the moon.

SONG

Take, O take those lips away,
　　That so sweetly were forsworn;
And those eyes, the break of day,
　　Lights that do mislead the morn!
But my kisses bring again,
　　　　　　bring again,
Seals of love, but seal'd in vain,
　　　　　seal'd in vain!

FAREWELL TO NANCY

Ae fond kiss, and then we sever;
Ae fareweel, alas, for ever!
Deep in heart-wrung tears I'll pledge thee,
Warring sighs and groans I'll wage thee!

Who shall say that Fortune grieves him
While the star of hope she leaves him?
Me, nae cheerfu' twinkle lights me,
Dark despair around benights me.

I'll ne'er blame my partial fancy;
Nothing could resist my Nancy;
But to see her was to love her,
Love but her, and love for ever.

Had we never loved sae kindly,
Had we never loved sae blindly,
Never met—or never parted,
We had ne'er been broken-hearted.

Fare thee weel, thou first and fairest!
Fare thee weel, thou best and dearest!
Thine be ilka joy and treasure,
Peace, enjoyment, love and pleasure!

Ae fond kiss, and then we sever!
Ae fareweel, alas, for ever!
Deep in heart-wrung tears I'll pledge thee,
Warring sighs and groans I'll wage thee!

A REVOCATION

What should I say,
    Since Faith is dead,
And Truth away
    From you is fled?
    Should I be led
        With doubleness?
        Nay, nay, mistress!

I promised you
    And you promised me,
To be as true,
    As I would be.
    But since I see
        Your double heart,
        Farewell my part!

Thought for to take
    'Tis not my mind;
But to forsake
    One so unkind;
    And as I find
        So will I trust.
        Farewell, unjust!

Can ye say nay,
    But that you said
That I alway
    Should be obeyed?
    And—thus betrayed,
        Ere that I wist,
        Farewell, unkist!

FROM *THE PRINCESS: II*

Ah, sad and strange, as in dark summer dawns
The earliest pipe of half-awaken'd birds
To dying ears, when unto dying eyes
The casement slowly grows a glimmering square;
So sad, so strange, the days that are no more.

Dear as remember'd kisses after death,
And sweet as those by hopeless fancy feign'd
On lips that are for others; deep as love,
Deep as first love and wild with all regret;
O Death in Life, the days that are no more!

WHEN WE TWO PARTED

When we two parted
　　In silence and tears,
Half broken-hearted
　　To sever for years,
Pale grew thy cheek and cold,
　　Colder thy kiss;
Truly that hour foretold
　　Sorrow to this.

The dew of the morning
　　Sunk chill on my brow—
It felt like the warning
　　Of what I feel now.
Thy vows are all broken,
　　And light is thy fame:
I hear thy name spoken,
　　And share in its shame.

They name thee before me,
　　A knell to mine ear;
A shudder comes o'er me—
　　Why wert thou so dear?
They know not I knew thee,
　　Who knew thee too well:
Long, long shall I rue thee,
　　Too deeply to tell.

In secret we met—
　　In silence I grieve,
That thy heart could forget,
　　Thy spirit deceive.

If I should meet thee
  After long years,
How should I greet thee?
  With silence and tears.

O MORS! QUAM AMARA EST
MEMORIA TUA HOMINI PACEM
HABENTI IN SUBSTANTIIS SUIS

Exceeding sorrow
   Consumeth my sad heart!
Because to-morrow
   We must depart,
Now is exceeding sorrow
   All my part!

Give over playing,
   Cast thy viol away:
Merely laying
   Thine head my way:
Prithee, give over playing,
   Grave or gay.

Be no word spoken,
   Weep nothing: let a pale
Silence, unbroken
   Silence, prevail!
Prithee, be no word spoken,
   Lest I fail!

Forget to-morrow.
   Weep nothing: only lay
In silent sorrow
   Thine head my way:
Let us forget to-morrow,
   This one day!

A HOPE FOR THOSE SEPARATED BY WAR

They crossed her face with blood,
They hung her heart.
They dragged her through a pit
Full of quick sorrow.
Yet her small feet
Ran back on the morrow.

They took his book and caged
His mind in a dark house.
They took his bright eyes
To light their rooms of doubt.
Yet his thin hands
Crawled back and found her out.

FELO DE SE

My heart's delight, I must for love forget you;
I must put you from my heart, the better to please you;
I must make the power of the spirit set you
Beyond the power of the mind to seize you.

My dearest heart, in this last act of homage,
I must reject you; I must unlearn to love you;
I must make my eyes give up your adorable image
And from the inner chamber of my soul remove you.

Heart of my heart, the heart alone has courage
Thus to relinquish; it is yourself that stills you
In all my pulses, and dissolves the marriage
Of soul and soul, and at the heart's core kills you.

RELUCTANCE

Out through the fields and the woods
And over the walls I have wended;
I have climbed the hills of view
And looked at the world, and descended;
I have come by the highway home,
And lo, it is ended.

The leaves are all dead on the ground,
   Save those that the oak is keeping
To ravel them one by one
   And let them go scraping and creeping
Out over the crusted snow
   When others are sleeping.

And the dead leaves lie huddled and still,
   No longer blown hither and thither;
The last lone aster is gone;
   The flowers of the witch hazel wither;
The heart is still aching to seek
   But the feet question "Whither?"

Ah, when to the heart of man
   Was it ever less than a treason
To go with the drift of things,
   To yield with a grace to reason,
And bow and accept the end
   Of a love or a season?

I GOT SO I COULD HEAR HIS NAME

I got so I could hear his name
Without—
Tremendous gain!—
That stop-sensation in my soul,
And thunder in the room.

I got so I could walk across
That angle in the floor
Where he turned—so—and I turned how—
And all our sinew tore.

I got so I could stir the box
In which his letters grew—
Without that forcing in my breath
As staples driven through.

Could dimly recollect a Grace—
I think they called it "God,"
Renowned to ease extremity
When formula had failed—

And shape my hands petition's way—
Tho' ignorant of word
That Ordination utters—
My business with the cloud.

If any Power behind it be
Not subject to despair,
To care in some remoter way
For so minute affair

As misery—
Itself too vast for interrupting more,
Supremer than—
Superior to—

SONNET

Night is my sister, and how deep in love,
How drowned in love and weedily washed ashore,
There to be fretted by the drag and shove
At the tide's edge, I lie—these things and more:
Whose arm alone between me and the sand,
Whose voice alone, whose pitiful breath brought near,
Could thaw these nostrils and unlock this hand,
She could advise you, should you care to hear.
Small chance, however, in a storm so black,
A man will leave his friendly fire and snug
For a drowned woman's sake, and bring her back
To drip and scatter shells upon the rug.
No one but Night, with tears on her dark face,
Watches beside me in this windy place.

PARTING

My life closed twice before its close;
    It yet remains to see
If Immortality unveil
    A third event to me,

So huge, so hopeless to conceive,
    As these that twice befell:
Parting is all we know of heaven,
    And all we need of hell.

ON FANNY GODWIN

Her voice did quiver as we parted,
    Yet knew I not that heart was broken
From which it came, and I departed
    Heeding not the words then spoken.
      Misery—O Misery,
      This world is all too wide for thee.

FROM *FÉLISE*

What shall be said between us here,
  Among the downs, between the trees,
In fields that knew our feet last year,
  In sight of quiet sands and seas,
  This year, Félise?

Who knows what word were best to say?
  For last year's leaves lie dead and red
On this sweet day, in this green May,
  And barren corn makes bitter bread,
  What shall be said?

Here as last year the fields begin,
  A fire of flowers and glowing grass;
The old fields we laughed and lingered in,
  Seeing each our souls in last year's glass,
  Félise, alas!

THE END OF THE EPISODE

Indulge no more may we
In this sweet-bitter pastime:
The love-light shines the last time
    Between you, Dear, and me.

There shall remain no trace
Of what so closely tied us,
And blank as ere love eyed us
    Will be our meeting-place.

The flowers and thymy air,
Will they now miss our coming?
The dumbles thin their humming
    To find we haunt not there?

Though fervent was our vow,
Though ruddily ran our pleasure,
Bliss has fulfilled its measure,
    And sees its sentence now.

Ache deep; but make no moans:
Smile out; but stilly suffer:
The paths of love are rougher
    Than thoroughfares of stones.

THE LAST WISH

Since all that I can ever do for thee
Is to do nothing, this my prayer must be:
That thou mayst never guess nor ever see
The all-endured this nothing-done costs me.

RENOUNCEMENT

I must not think of thee; and, tired yet strong,
I shun the thought that lurks in all delight—
   The thought of thee—and in the blue Heaven's height,
And in the sweetest passage of a song.

Oh, just beyond the fairest thoughts that throng
   This breast, the thought of thee waits, hidden yet bright;
But it must never, never come in sight;
I must stop short of thee the whole day long.

But when sleep comes to close each difficult day,
   When night gives pause to the long watch I keep,
And all my bonds I needs must loose apart,

Must doff my will as raiment laid away,—
   With the first dream that comes with the first sleep
I run, I run, I am gathered to thy heart.

FAREWELL!

Farewell! if ever fondest prayer
  For other's weal availed on high,
Mine will not all be lost in air,
  But waft thy name beyond the sky.
'Twere vain to speak, to weep, to sigh:
  Oh! more than tears of blood can tell,
When wrung from guilt's expiring eye,
    Are in that word—Farewell!—Farewell!

These lips are mute, these eyes are dry;
  But in my breast and in my brain,
Awake the pangs that pass not by,
  The thought that ne'er shall sleep again.
My soul nor deigns nor dares complain,
  Though grief and passion there rebel;
I only know we loved in vain—
    I only feel—Farewell!—Farewell!

SONG TO A VIOL

So the silver-feathered swan,
Both by death and colour wan,
Loves to sing before she die,
Leaving life so willingly.
But how can I sing a note
When dead hoarseness stops my throat?
Or how can I play a stroke
When my heart-strings are all broke?

FORGET NOT YET

Forget not yet the tried intent
Of such a truth as I have meant;
My great travail so gladly spent
Forget not yet!

Forget not yet when first began
The weary life ye know, since whan
The suit, the service none tell can;
Forget not yet!

Forget not yet the great assays,
The cruel wrong, the scornful ways,
The painful patience in denays,
Forget not yet!

Forget not, oh! forget not this,
How long ago hath been, and is
The mind that never meant amiss—
Forget not yet!

Forget not then thine own approved,
The which so long hath thee so loved,
Whose steadfast faith yet never moved,
Forget not this!

THOU FLOWER OF SUMMER

When in summer thou walkest
  In the meads by the river,
And to thyself talkest,
  Dost thou think of one ever—
A lost and a lorn one
  That adores thee and loves thee?
And when happy morn's gone,
  And nature's calm moves thee,
Leaving thee to thy sleep like an angel at rest,
Does the one who adores thee still live in thy breast?

Does nature e'er give thee
  Love's past happy vision,
And wrap thee and leave thee
  In fancies Elysian?
Thy beauty I clung to,
  As leaves to the tree;
When thou, fair and young too,
  Looked lightly on me,
Till love came upon thee like the sun to the west
And shed its perfuming and bloom on thy breast.

ROSE AYLMER

Ah, what avails the sceptred race!
   Ah, what the form divine!
What every virtue, every grace!
   Rose Aylmer, all were thine.

Rose Aylmer, whom these wakeful eyes
   May weep, but never see,
A night of memories and of sighs
   I consecrate to thee.

TWO WAYS

Oncet in the museum
 We seen a little rose
In a jar of alcohol—
 You turns up your nose:
"That's the way people think
 Love ought to be—
Last forever! Pickled roses!—
 None o' that for me!"

That night was fireworks
 Out to Riverview—
Gold and red and purple
 Bustin' over you.
"Beautiful!" you says then,
 "That's how love should be!
Burn wild and die quick—
 That's the love for me!"

Now you're gone for good . . . say,
Wasn't they no other way?

SONNET CII

My love is strengthen'd, though more weak in seeming;
I love not less, though less the show appear:
That love is merchandised, whose rich esteeming
The owner's tongue doth publish every where.
Our love was new, and then but in the spring,
When I was wont to greet it with my lays,
As Philomel in summer's front doth sing,
And stops her pipe in growth of riper days:
Not that the summer is less pleasant now
Than when her mournful hymns did hush the night,
But that wild music burthens every bough,
And sweets grown common lose their dear delight.
  Therefore, like her, I sometime hold my tongue,
  Because I would not dull you with my song.

AWAY, YOUR TOUCH IS EVERYWHERE

Away, your touch is everywhere.
The books like fever call your cooling name;
the telephone leaps with the claws of a cat,
scratch vainly on unanswer.

The dishes fall down of themselves,
refuse to be swept together
and the clock in deshabille
says Why should I bother to dress?

While all the deadlong day I work
to scrub the telltale marks away
of How you looked and What you said:
like tattoo, like murder, the mark.

Exhausted in bed each night
surrounded by all we own,
to lie alone in our double home
a salesman in a rented room.

CROWNED

You came to me bearing bright roses,
  Red like the wine of your heart;
You twisted them into a garland
  To set me aside from the mart.
Red roses to crown me your lover,
  And I walked aureoled and apart.

Enslaved and encircled, I bore it,
  Proud token of my gift to you.
The petals waned paler, and shriveled,
  And dropped; and the thorns started through.
Bitter thorns to proclaim me your lover,
  A diadem woven with rue.

LET IT BE FORGOTTEN

Let it be forgotten, as a flower is forgotten,
　　Forgotten as a fire that once was singing gold.
Let it be forgotten forever and ever,
　　Time is a kind friend, he will make us old.

If anyone asks, say it was forgotten
　　Long and long ago,
As a flower, as a fire, as a hushed footfall
　　In a long-forgotten snow.

HEART, WE WILL FORGET HIM!

Heart, we will forget him!
  You and I, to-night!
You may forget the warmth he gave,
  I will forget the light.

When you have done, pray tell me,
  That I my thoughts may dim;
Haste! lest while you're lagging,
  I may remember him!

PITY ME NOT

Pity me not because the light of day
At close of day no longer walks the sky;
Pity me not for beauties passed away
From field and thicket as the year goes by;
Pity me not the waning of the moon,
Nor that the ebbing tide goes out to sea,
Nor that a man's desire is hushed so soon,
And you no longer look with love on me.
This have I known always; love is no more
Than the wide blossom which the wind assails,
Than the great tide that treads the shifting shore,
Strewing fresh wreckage gathered in the gales:
Pity me that the heart is slow to learn
What the swift mind beholds at every turn.

SOMETIMES WITH ONE I LOVE

Sometimes with one I love I fill myself with rage for fear
I effuse unreturn'd love,
But now I think there is no unreturn'd love, the pay is certain
one way or another.
(I loved a certain person ardently, and my love was not
return'd,
Yet out of that I have written these songs.)

FROM *THE EXEQUY*

Sleep on, my Love, in thy cold bed
Never to be disquieted!
My last good-night! Thou wilt not wake
Till I thy fate shall overtake:
Till age, or grief, or sickness must
Marry my body to that dust
It so much loves; and fill the room
My heart keeps empty in thy tomb.
Stay for me there! I will not fail
To meet thee in that hollow vale.
And think not much of my delay:
I am already on the way,
And follow thee with all the speed
Desire can make, or sorrows breed.
Each minute is a short degree,
And every hour a step towards thee.
At night when I betake to rest,
Next morn I rise nearer my west
Of life, almost by eight hours' sail,
Than when sleep breathed his drowsy gale.

ANNIVERSARY

That was a kindly storm, I know,
That leaned against the ship's strong side,
That held me from you while you died.
The sea is not as salt, as wide,
As is such human woe.

Shallow the ocean, tempest tame!...
They say you called the far ship's name,
They say that Tristram did the same.

LOVE CAME BACK AT FALL O' DEW

Love came back at fall o' dew,
Playing his old part;
But I had a word or two
That would break his heart.

"He who comes at candle-light,
That should come before,
Must betake him to the night
From a barrèd door."

This the word that made us part
In the fall o' dew;
This the word that brake his heart—
Yet it brake mine, too.

DOUGLAS

Could ye come back to me, Douglas, Douglas,
   In the old likeness that I knew,
I would be so faithful, so loving, Douglas,
   Douglas, Douglas, tender and true.

Never a scornful word should grieve ye,
   I'd smile on ye sweet as the angels do:
Sweet as your smile on me shone ever,
   Douglas, Douglas, tender and true!

O, to call back the days that are not!
   My eyes were blinded, your words were few:
Do you know the truth now up in heaven,
   Douglas, Douglas, tender and true?

I never was worthy of you, Douglas;
   Not half worthy the like of you;
Now all men beside seem to me like shadows—
   I love *you,* Douglas, tender and true.

Stretch out your hand to me, Douglas, Douglas,
   Drop forgiveness from heaven like dew,
As I lay my heart on your dead heart, Douglas,
   Douglas, Douglas, tender and true!

FROM *MAUD PART II*

O that 'twere possible
After long grief and pain
To find the arms of my true love
Round me once again!...

A shadow flits before me,
Not thou but like to thee:
Ah, Christ! that it were possible
For one short hour to see
The souls we loved, that they might tell us
What and where they be!

REMEMBRANCE

Cold in the earth—and the deep snow piled above thee,
Far, far removed, cold in the dreary grave!
Have I forgot, my only Love, to love thee,
Severed at last by Time's all-wearing wave?

Now, when alone, do my thoughts no longer hover
Over the mountains, on Angora's shore,
Resting their wings where heath and fern-leaves cover
That noble heart for ever, ever more?

Cold in the earth, and fifteen wild Decembers
From those brown hills, have melted into spring:
Faithful, indeed, is the spirit that remembers
After such years of change and suffering!

Sweet Love of youth, forgive, if I forget thee,
While the world's tide is bearing me along;
Sterner desires and darker hopes beset me,
Hopes which obscure, but cannot do thee wrong!

No other sun has lightened up my heaven,
No other star has ever shone for me;
All my life's bliss from thy dear life was given,
All my life's bliss is in the grave with thee.

But, when the days of golden dreams had perished,
And even Despair was powerless to destroy;
Then did I learn how existence could be cherished,
Strengthened and fed without the aid of joy.

Then did I check the tears of useless passion—
Weaned my young soul from yearning after thine;

Sternly denied its burning wish to hasten
Down to that tomb already more than mine.

And, even yet, I dare not let it languish,
Dare not indulge in memory's rapturous pain:
Once drinking deep of that divinest anguish.
How could I seek the empty world again?

THE RETURN

A little hand is knocking at my heart,
And I have closed the door.
"I pray thee, for the love of God, depart:
Thou shalt come in no more."

"Open, for I am weary of the way.
The night is very black.
I have been wandering many a night and day.
Open. I have come back."

The little hand is knocking patiently;
I listen, dumb with pain.
"Wilt thou not open any more to me?
I have come back again."

"I will not open any more. Depart.
I, that once lived, am dead."
The hand that had been knocking at my heart
Was still. "And I?" she said.

There is no sound, save, in the winter air,
The sound of wind and rain.
All that I loved in all the world stands there,
And will not knock again.

FROM *LES NOYADES*

Could I change you, help you to love me, sweet,
    Could I give you the love that would sweeten death,
We should yield, go down, locked hands and feet,
    Die, drown together, and breath catch breath;

But you would have felt my soul in a kiss,
    And known that once if I loved you well;
And I would have given my soul for this
    To burn for ever in burning hell.

FROM *EPIPSYCHIDION*

Spouse! Sister! Angel! Pilot of the Fate!
Whose course has been so starless! O too late
Belovèd! O too soon adored, by me!
For in the fields of immortality
My spirit should at first have worshipped thine,
A divine presence in a place divine;
Or should have moved beside it on this earth,
A shadow of that substance, from its birth;
But not as now:—I love thee; yes, I feel
That on the fountain of my heart a seal
Is set, to keep its waters pure and bright
For thee, since in those *tears* thou hast delight.
We—are we not formed, as notes of music are,
For one another, though dissimilar;
Such difference without discord, as can make
Those sweetest sounds, in which all spirits shake
As trembling leaves in a continuous air?

WHERE, O, WHERE?

I need not die to go
So far you cannot know
My escape, my retreat,
And the prints of my feet
Written in blood or dew;
They shall be hid from you,
In fern-seed lost
Or the soft flakes of frost.
They will turn somewhere
Under water, over air,
To earth space or stellar,
Or the garret or cellar
Of the house next door;
You shall see me no more
Though each night I hide
In your bed, at your side.

THE MARRIED LOVER

Why, having won her, do I woo?
  Because her spirit's vestal grace
Provokes me always to pursue,
  But, spirit-like, eludes embrace; ...

Because, although in act and word
  As lowly as a wife can be,
Her manners, when they call me lord,
  Remind me 'tis by courtesy; ...

Because her gay and lofty brows,
  When all is won which hope can ask,
Reflect a light of hopeless snows,
  That bright in virgin ether bask;

Because, though free of the outer court
  I am, this Temple keeps its shrine
Sacred to Heaven; because, in short,
  She's not and never can be mine.

IF I AM BUT THE WATER

If I am but the water
That lies within your banks,
How peacefully you hold me in,
And with how little thanks,
For all my petty torrents
That thunderstorms create,
Are harbored in your holding earth
Untroubled by my spate.
If years have served to deepen
The waters you contain,
They may the more reflect your joy
And cover up your pain,
And if my waters gather
To turn a splendid wheel,
It will be you that locked its power
And you that broke its seal.

LA FIGLIA CHE PIANGE

Stand on the highest pavement of the stair—
Lean on a garden urn—
Weave, weave, weave the sunlight in your hair—
Clasp your flowers to you with pained surprise—
Fling them to the ground and turn
With a fugitive resentment in your eyes:
But weave, weave the sunlight in your hair.

So I would have him leave,
So I would have her stand and grieve,
So he would have left
As the soul leaves the body torn and bruised,
As the mind deserts the body it has used.
I should find
Some way incomparably light and deft,
Some way we both should understand,
Simple and faithless as a smile and shake of the hand.

She turned away, but with the autumn weather
Compelled my imagination many days,
Many days and many hours:
Her hair over her arms and her arms full of flowers.
And I wonder how they should have been together!
I should have lost a gesture and a pose.
Sometimes these cogitations still amaze
The troubled midnight and the noon's repose.

MELILOT

Behind the house is the millet plot,
And past the millet, the stile;
And then a hill where melilot
Grows with wild camomile.

There was a youth who bade me goodby
Where the hill rises to meet the sky.
I think my heart broke; but I have forgot
All but the scent of the white melilot.

V. MATURITY

To think how little I dreamed it led
To an age so blest that, by its side,
Youth seems the waste instead?

—ROBERT BROWNING

THE VINE

The wine of Love is music,
    And the feast of Love is song:
And when Love sits down to the banquet,
    Love sits long:

Sits long and arises drunken,
    But not with the feast and the wine;
He reeleth with his own heart,
    That great, rich Vine.

FROM *THE GARDEN IN SEPTEMBER*

So sweet love seemed that April morn,
When first we kissed beside the thorn,
So strangely sweet it was not strange
We thought that love could never change.

But I can tell—let truth be told—
That love will change in growing old;
Though day by day is nought to see,
So delicate his motions be.

And in the end 'twill come to pass
Quite to forget what once he was,
Nor even in fancy to recall
The pleasure that was all in all.

His little spring, that sweet we found,
So deep in summer floods is drowned,
I wonder, bathed in joy complete,
How love so young could be so sweet.

ROMANCE

I will make you brooches and toys for your delight
Of bird-song at morning and star-shine at night.
I will make a palace fit for you and me,
Of green days in forests and blue days at sea.

I will make my kitchen and you shall keep your room
Where white flows the river and bright blows the broom,
And you shall wash your linen and keep your body white
In rainfall at morning and dewfall at night.

And this shall be for music when no one else is near,
The fine song for singing, the rare song to hear!
That only I remember, that only you admire,
Of the broad road that stretches and the roadside fire.

TO ROSEMARY

If you were gone afar,
And lost the pattern
Of your delightful ways,
And the web undone,
How would one make you anew,
From what dew and flowers,
What burning and mingled atoms,
Under the sun?

Not from too-satin roses,
Or those rare blossoms,
Orchids, scentless and precious
As precious stone.
But out of lemon-verbena,
Rose-geranium.
These alone.

Not with running horses,
Or Spanish cannon.
Organs, voiced like a lion,
Clamor and speed.
But perhaps with old music-boxes,
Young, tawny kittens,
Wild-strawberry-seed.

Even so, it were more
Than a god could compass
To fashion the body merely,
The lovely shroud.
But then—ah, how to recapture
That evanescence,
The fire that cried in pure crystal
Out of its cloud.

LOVE'S VISION

There is no happy life
But in a wife;
The comforts are so sweet
When they do meet:
'Tis plenty, peace, a calm
Like dropping balm:
Love's weather is so fair,
Perfumèd air,
Each word such pleasure brings
Like soft-touched strings;
Love's passion moves the heart
On either part.
Such harmony together,
So pleased in either,
No discords, concords still,
Sealed with one will.
By love, God made man one,
Yet not alone:
Like stamps of king and queen
It may be seen,
Two figures but one coin;
So they do join,
Only they not embrace,
We face to face.

POEM IN PROSE

This poem is for my wife
I have made it plainly and honestly
The mark is on it
Like the burl on the knife

I have not made it for praise
She has no more need for praise
Than summer has
Or the bright days

In all that becomes a woman
Her words and her ways are beautiful
Love's lovely duty
The well-swept room

Wherever she is there is sun
And time and a sweet air
Peace is there
Work done

There are always curtains and flowers
And candles and baked bread
And a cloth spread
And a clean house

Her voice when she sings is a voice
At dawn by a freshening sea
Where the wave leaps in the
Wind and rejoices

Wherever she is it is now
It is here where the apples are
Here in the stars
In the quick hour

The greatest and richest good—
My own life to live in—
This she has given me

If giver could.

THE FOLLY OF BEING COMFORTED

One that is ever kind said yesterday:
'Your well-belovèd's hair has threads of grey,
And little shadows come about her eyes;
Time can but make it easier to be wise
Though now it seems impossible, and so
All that you need is patience.'
                Heart cries, 'No,
I have not a crumb of comfort, not a grain,
Time can but make her beauty over again:
Because of that great nobleness of hers
The fire that stirs about her, when she stirs,
Burns but more clearly. O she had not these ways,
When all the wild summer was in her gaze.'
O heart! O heart! if she'd but turn her head,
You'd know the folly of being comforted.

BEAUTY

I have seen dawn and sunset on moors and windy hills
Coming in solemn beauty like slow old tunes of Spain:
I have seen the lady April bringing the daffodils,
Bringing the springing grass and the soft warm, April rain.

I have heard the song of the blossoms and the old chant of the
 sea,
And seen strange lands from under the arched white sails of
 ships;
But the loveliest things of beauty God ever has shown to me
Are her voice, and her hair, and eyes, and the dear red curve
 of her lips.

FROM
WOMEN BEWARE OF WOMEN: A TRAGEDY

'... How near am I now to a happiness
That earth exceeds not! Not another like it:
The treasures of the deep are not so precious,
As are the conceal'd comforts of a man
Lock'd up in woman's love. I scent the air
Of blessings when I come but near the house:
What a delicious breath marriage sends forth!
The violet-bed's not sweeter! Honest wedlock
Is like a banqueting-house built in a garden,
On which the spring's chaste flowers take delight
To cast their modest odours; when base lust,
With all her powder, paintings, and pert pride,
Is but a fair house built by a ditch-side...'

TWO SONNETS:

I. YEA

It was beside the fire that I had lit,
Out of the rain that drummed upon my roof,
She leant against my bosom, fluttering it,
And stared beyond my world: far, far aloof.

And neither spake, and thus we might have sat
Till angry Gabriel trumpeted for change,
But she said: "Heart of stone, look not like that!
O unconcessive husband, you are strange."

For joy I could not answer, being taxed
By such a star, so distant in the sky,
With being cold. But think how the poor heart waxed,
This chidden wonder of women, the huge I!

And I played the god; disdaining her no more
I smiled, and drew her closer than before.

HUSBAND AND WIFE

Not theirs the vain, tumultuous bliss,
Whose only currency's a kiss,
Nor linkèd hands, nor meeting eyes,
But long-drawn mutual silences,
Community in trivial things,
The rare fantastic mood that brings
Wisdom and mirth unspeakable
Out of an insect or a shell.

I REMEMBERED

There never was a mood of mine,
   Gay or heart-broken, luminous or dull,
But you could ease me of its fever
   And give it back to me more beautiful.

In many another soul I broke the bread,
   And drank the wine and played the happy guest,
But I was lonely, I remembered you;
   The heart belongs to him who knew it best.

SONG

Since thou, O fondest and truest,
Hast loved me best and longest,
And now with trust the strongest
The joy of my heart renewest;

Since thou art dearer and dearer
While other hearts grow colder
And ever, as love is older,
More lovingly drawest nearer:

Since now I see in the measure
Of all my giving and taking,
Thou wert my hand in the making,
The sense and soul of my pleasure;

The good I have ne'er repaid thee
In heaven I pray be recorded,
And all thy love rewarded
By God, thy master that made thee.

PROPER CLAY

Their little room grew light with cries;
He woke and heard them thread the dark,
He woke and felt them like the rays
Of some unlawful dawn at work:

Some random sunrise, lost and small,
That found the room's heart, vein by vein.
But she was whispering to the wall,
And he must see what she had seen.

He asked her gently, and she wept.
"Oh, I have dreamed the ancient dream.
My time was on me, and I slept;
And I grew greater than I am;

"And lay like dead; but when I lived,
Three wingèd midwives wrapped the child.
It was a god that I had loved,
It was a hero I had held.

"Stretch out your mortal hands, I beg.
Say common sentences to me.
Lie cold and still, that I may brag
How close I am to proper clay.

"Let this within me hear the truth.
Speak loud to it." He stopped her lips.
He smoothed the covers over both.
It was a dream perhaps, perhaps,

Yet why this radiance round the room,
And why this trembling at her waist?
And then he smiled. It was the same
Undoubted flesh that he had kissed;

She lay unchanged from what she was,
She cried as ever woman cried.
Yet why this light along his brows?
And whence the music no one made?

A DECADE

When you came, you were like red wine and honey,
And the taste of you burnt my mouth with its sweetness.
Now you are like morning bread,
Smooth and pleasant.
I hardly taste you at all, for I know your savor;
But I am completely nourished.

FROM *BY THE FIRESIDE*

With me youth led ... I will speak now,
   No longer watch you as you sit
Reading by firelight, that great brow
   And the spirit small hand propping it,
Mutely, my heart knows how—

When, if I think but deep enough,
   You are wont to answer, prompt as rhyme;
And you, too, find without rebuff
   Response your soul seeks many a time
Piercing its fine flesh-stuff.

My own, confirm me! If I tread
   This path back, is it not in pride
To think how little I dreamed it led
   To an age so blest that, by its side,
Youth seems the waste instead?

My own, see where the years conduct!
   At first, 'twas something our two souls
Should mix as mists do; each is sucked
   In each now: on the new stream rolls,
Whatever rocks obstruct.

Think, when our one soul understands
   The great Word which makes all things new,
When earth breaks up and heaven expands,
   How will the change strike me and you
In the house not made with hands?

Oh, I must feel your brain prompt mine,
   Your heart anticipate my heart,
You must be just before, in fine,
   See and make me see, for your part,
New depths of the divine!

But who could have expected this
   When we two drew together first
Just for the obvious human bliss,
   To satisfy life's daily thirst
With a thing men seldom miss?

．　．　．　．　．　．

I am named and known by that moment's feat;
   There took my station and degree;
So grew my own small life complete,
   As Nature obtained her best of me—
One born to love you, sweet!

And to watch you sink by the fireside now
   Back again, as you mutely sit
Musing by firelight, that great brow
   And the spirit-small hand propping it,
Yonder, my heart knows how!

So, earth has gained by one man the more,
   And the gain of earth must be heaven's gain, too;
And the whole is well worth thinking o'er
   When autumn comes; which I mean to do
One day, as I said before.

VI. LOVE'S IMMORTALITY

There will be stars over the place forever,
There will be stars forever while we sleep.

—SARA TEASDALE

FROM *SONNETS FROM THE PORTUGUESE*

If thou must love me, let it be for naught
Except for love's sake only. Do not say,
"I love her for her smile—her look—her way
Of speaking gently—for a trick of thought
That falls in well with mine, and certes brought
A sense of pleasant ease on such a day"—
For these things in themselves, Belovèd, may
Be changed, or change for thee—and love, so wrought,
May be unwrought so. Neither love me for
Thine own dear pity's wiping my cheeks dry:
A creature might forget to weep, who bore
Thy comfort long, and lose thy love thereby!
But love me for love's sake, that evermore
Thou may'st love on, through love's eternity.

TRAGIC LOVE

Who shall invoke when we are gone
  The glory that we knew,
Can we not carve To-day in stone,
  In diamond this dawn's dew?

The song that heart to heart has sung
  Write fadeless on the air;
Expression in eyes briefly hung
  Fix in a planet's stare?

Alas, all beauty flies in *Time*
  And only as it goes
Upon death's wind its fleeting chime
  Into sad memory blows.

Is this but presage of re-birth
  And of another Day
When what within our hearts we said
  We once again shall say?

Oh, no! we never could repeat
  Those numbered looks we gave;
But some pure lustre from their light
  All future worlds shall have.

THE WHITE DRESS

Some evening when you are sitting alone,
   by your high window, motionless and white—
I shall come, by the way that none but I have known,
   into the quiet room out of the night.

You will know I have come, without turning your head
   because of the way the air will lie quite still,
as though it waited for something to be said
   that no man has ever said, and no man will.

But you will be wiser than the air. You know
   that for the thing we feel there is no word—
and you will not move even when I turn to go,
   even when the sound of my footsteps is no longer heard.

INSCRIPTION FOR A MIRROR
IN A DESERTED DWELLING

Set silver cone to tulip flame!
The mantel mirror floats with night
Reflecting still green watery light.
The sconces glimmer. If she came
Like silence through the shadowy wall
Where walls are wading in the moon
The dark would tremble back to June.
So faintly now the moonbeams fall,
So soft this silence, that the verge
Of speech is reached. Remote and pale
As through some faint viridian veil
The lovely lineaments emerge,
The clearly amber eyes, the tint
Of pearl and faintest rose, the hair
To lacquered light, a silken snare
Of devious bronze, the tiny dint
With which her maker mocked the years
Beneath her lip imprinting praise.
Dim flower of desecrating days,
The old reflection, strange with tears,
Is gazing out upon the gloom,
Is widening eyes to find the light
In reminiscence, in the night
Of this foregone, forgotten room.
And you, the watcher, with your eyes
As wide as hers in dark distress,
Who never knew her loveliness
But guess through glass her shadowy guise,
For you around the glass I trace
This secret writing, that will burn
Like witch-fire should her shade return

To haunt you with that wistful face.
At least no gesturing figures pass;
Here is no tragic immanence
Of all the scenes of small events
That pantomimed before the glass.
No bliss, no passion, no despair,
No other actor lingers now;
The moonlight on a lifted brow
Is all,—the eyes so wide aware
Of clouds that pass with stars, and suns,
Of mystery that pales the cheek,
Of all the heart could never speak,
Of joy and pain so vivid once,
That ceased with music and the lights,
Dimming to darkness and repose...
Lean then and kiss that ghostly rose
That was her face, this night of nights,—
And know the vision fled indeed,
The mirror's surface smooth and cold,
The words unbreathed, the tale untold,
The past unpiteous to your need!

THERE WILL BE STARS

There will be stars over the place forever;
   Though the house we loved and the street we loved are lost,
Every time the earth circles her orbit
   On the night the autumn equinox is crossed,
Two stars we knew, poised on the peak of midnight,
   Will reach their zenith; stillness will be deep;
There will be stars over the place forever,
   There will be stars forever, while we sleep.

"I NEED NOT GO"

I need not go
Through sleet and snow
To where I know
She waits for me;
She will tarry me there
Till I find it fair,
And have time to spare
From company.

When I've overgot
The world somewhat,
When things cost not
Such stress and strain,
Is soon enough
By cypress sough
To tell my Love
I am come again.

And if some day,
When none cries nay,
I still delay
To seek her side,
(Though ample measure
Of fitting leisure
Await my pleasure)
She will not chide.

What—not upbraid me
That I delay'd me,
Nor ask what stay'd me
So long? Ah, no!—

New cares may claim me.
New loves inflame me,
She will not blame me,
But suffer it so.

FROM *SONNETS FROM THE PORTUGUESE*

Go from me. Yet I feel that I shall stand
Henceforward in thy shadow. Nevermore
Alone upon the threshold of my door
Of individual life I shall command
The uses of my soul, nor lift my hand
Serenely in the sunshine as before,
Without the sense of that which I forbore—
Thy touch upon the palm. The widest land
Doom takes to part us, leaves thy heart in mine
With pulses that beat double. What I do
And what I dream include thee, as the wine
Must taste of its own grapes. And when I sue
God for myself, He hears that name of thine,
And sees within my eyes the tears of two.

MY LIGHT WITH YOURS

When the sea has devoured the ships,
And the spires and the towers
Have gone back to the hills,
And all the cities are one with the plains again,
And the beauty of bronze
And the strength of steel
Are blown over silent continents,
As the desert sand is blown—
My dust with yours forever.

When folly and wisdom are no more,
And fire is no more,
Because man is no more;
When the dead world slowly spinning
Drifts and falls through the void—
My light with yours
In the Light of Lights forever!

SONGS ASCENDING

Love has been sung a thousand ways—
    So let it be;
The songs ascending in your praise
Through all my days
    Are three.

Your cloud-white body first I sing;
    Your love was heaven's blue,
And I, a bird, flew carolling
In ring on ring
    Of you.

Your nearness is the second song;
    When God began to be,
And bound you strongly, right or wrong,
With his own thong,
    To me.

But oh, the song eternal, high
    That tops these two!—
You live forever, you who die,
I am not I
    But you.

TWO SONNETS: II

Now is Death merciful. He calls me hence
Gently, with friendly soothing of my fears
Of ugly age and feeble impotence
And cruel disintegration of slow years.
Nor does he leap upon me unaware
Like some wild beast that hungers for its prey,
But gives me kindly warning to prepare
Before I go, to kiss your tears away.

How sweet the summer! And the autumn shone
Late warmth within our hearts as in the sky,
Ripening rich harvest that our love had sown.
How good that ere the winter comes, I die!
Then, ageless, in your heart I'll come to rest
Serene and proud as when you loved me best.

NIGHT

Celia, when you bade me
Good morning, I would wake
Quick again on your account,
Eager for your sake.

Yet at morning or at noon
In the clearest light
Is there any voice as near
As your voice at night?

Or has anyone alive
Ever come and said
Anything as intimate
As you are saying, dead?

THE DOOR

Love is a proud and gentle thing, a better thing to own
Than all of the wild impossible stars over the heavens blown,
And the little gifts her hand gives are careless given or taken,
And though the whole great world break, the heart of her is
    not shaken...

Love is a viol in the wind, a viol never stilled,
And mine of all is the surest that ever God has willed.
I shall speak to her though she goes before me into the grave,
And though I drown in the sea, herself shall laugh upon a
    wave;
And the things that love gives after shall be as they were
    before,
For life is only a small house... and love is an open door.

DISCORDANTS

I.

Music I heard with you was more than music,
And bread I broke with you was more than bread;
Now that I am without you, all is desolate;
All that was once so beautiful is dead.

Your hands once touched this table and this silver,
And I have seen your fingers hold this glass.
These things do not remember you, beloved,
And yet your touch upon them will not pass.

For it was in my heart you moved among them,
And blessed them with your hands and with your eyes;
And in my heart they will remember always,—
They knew you once, O beautiful and wise.

WHEN THE ROSE IS FADED

When the rose is faded,
   Memory may still dwell on
Her beauty shadowed,
   And the sweet smell gone.

The vanishing loveliness,
   That burdening breath,
No bond of life hath then,
   Nor grief of death.

'Tis the immortal thought
   Whose passion still
Makes of the changing
   The unchangeable.

Oh, thus thy beauty,
   Loveliest on earth to me,
Dark with no sorrow, shines
   And burns, with thee.

THE DARK CHAMBER

The brain forgets, but the blood will remember.
There, when the play of sense is over,
The last low spark in the darkest chamber
Will hold all there is of love and lover.

The war of words, the life-long quarrel
Of self against self will resolve into nothing;
Less than the chain of berry-red coral
Crying against the dead black of her clothing.

What has the brain that it hopes to last longer?
The blood will take from forgotten violence,
The groping, the break of her voice in anger.
There will be left only color and silence.

These will remain, these will go searching
Your veins for life when the flame of life smoulders:
The night that you two saw the mountains marching
Up against dawn with the stars on their shoulders—

The jetting poplars' arrested fountains
As you drew her under them, easing her pain—
The notes, not the words, of a half-finished sentence—
The music, the silence. . . . These will remain.

TO ONE IN PARADISE

Thou wast all that to me, love,
  For which my soul did pine—
A green isle in the sea, love,
  A fountain and a shrine,
All wreathed with fairy fruits and flowers,
  And all the flowers were mine.

Ah, dream too bright to last!
  Ah, starry Hope! that didst arise
But to be overcast!
  A voice from out the Future cries,
'On! on!'—but o'er the Past
  (Dim gulf!) my spirit hovering lies
Mute, motionless, aghast!

For, alas! alas! with me
  The light of Life is o'er!
No more—no more—no more—
  (Such language holds the solemn sea
To the sands upon the shore)—
  Shall bloom the thunder-blasted tree,
Or the stricken eagle soar!

And all my days are trances,
  And all my nightly dreams
Are where thy grey eye glances,
  And where thy footstep gleams—
In what ethereal dances,
  By what eternal streams.

ECHO

Come to me in the silence of the night;
  Come in the speaking silence of a dream;
Come with soft-rounded cheeks and eyes as bright
    As sunlight on a stream;
      Come back in tears,
O memory, hope, love of finished years.

O dream how sweet, too sweet, too bitter sweet,
  Whose wakening should have been in Paradise,
Where souls brimful of love abide and meet;
    Where thirsting longing eyes
      Watch the slow door
That opening, letting in, lets out no more.

Yet come to me in dreams, that I may live
  My very life again though cold in death:
Come back to me in dreams, that I may give
    Pulse for pulse, breath for breath:
      Speak low, lean low,
As long ago, my love, how long ago!

INDEX OF FIRST LINES